Augmented Communication

Richard S. Pinner

Augmented Communication

The Effect of Digital Devices on Face-to-Face
Interactions

palgrave
macmillan

Richard S. Pinner
Department of English Literature
Sophia University
Tokyo, Japan

ISBN 978-3-030-02079-8   ISBN 978-3-030-02080-4   (eBook)
https://doi.org/10.1007/978-3-030-02080-4

Library of Congress Control Number: 2018957437

This Palgrave Pivot imprint is published by the registered company Springer Nature
Switzerland AG
The registered company address is: Gewerbestrasse 11, 6330 Cham, Switzerland

ACKNOWLEDGEMENTS

I wish to thank all those who helped me with this inquiry. This book is thanks to the cooperation of so many people. My family, friends (both old and new) and students have all kindly given permission to discuss my observations. Thanks to everyone for your contributions.

I would especially like to mention Brandon Stanton from Humans of New York for kindly granting permission to use his photograph. I would also like to thank Beth Farrow at Palgrave Macmillan, who has been very supportive and enthusiastic during the writing of this book, and also consolidated me when appropriate. I would also like to thank my students who participated in the workgroup discussions, and especially Ai F for allowing me to use her photo. Of course, I could not have done this without the help and support of my family. Not just Kimie and Oscar but also my parents (and my Dad's friends!) and my sisters who have all helped in collecting the data and helping to make sense of this inquiry.

CONTENTS

1 Introduction   1

2 History of Augmented Communication: Technology
  and Disability   21

3 Augmented Communication as a Modern Phenomenon
  in Ordinary Speech   29

4 Types of Augmented Communication   49

5 Stepping Back: Analysis and Discussion of ICT
  and Language Change   87

6 Conclusion   123

Index   129

LIST OF FIGURES

Fig. 1.1	From HONY Facebook page 16 September 2015	4
Fig. 3.1	Picture taken during my talk in Kyoto and live-Tweeted	34
Fig. 3.2	FaceJuggler	37
Fig. 3.3	My father and his friends use Google Maps to talk about a new house	44
Fig. 4.1	Augmenting in Buenos Aires	53
Fig. 4.2	Augmenting in Tokyo	54
Fig. 4.3	Lookalike	58
Fig. 4.4	Friends become 'friends'	67
Fig. 4.5	Augmented participation	78
Fig. 5.1	Sumahobusu	107
Fig. 5.2	Japanese kindergarten—look with your own eyes	111
Fig. 5.3	Life or smartphone	112
Fig. 5.4	No Wifi as a selling point	113

ABSTRACT

There have been many studies and wider discourses surrounding the issues of technology influencing language. One of the most widely debated areas to arise recently is the idea that smartphones are having a detrimental effect on face-to-face communication. This book takes a markedly different approach in framing this phenomenon as augmented communication. People around the world are using handheld networked devices to enhance their face-to-face interactions. Utilising ethnographic and autoethnographic observation data, this book outlines how augmented communication is employed to enhance face-to-face communication. This book examines the way augmented communication alters face-to-face interactions by adding visual and multimodal input, by providing the speaker with access to online search engines, and by allowing the speaker to include others in the discussion from distant geographical locations, either synchronously or asynchronously. Using our phones, people draw on networked stores of information, which could be seen as a form of exomemory. Utilising skills and blended digital literacies to access and apply this is a new development in the way humans communicate. Augmented communication has arisen as a natural by-product of having access to such technology, a by-product of our polymediated age, and something yet to be explored in-depth from a sociolinguistic perspective. This book presents research data spanning several years of observation whilst indicating the possible consequences of such technology-enhanced interactions, and explores some of the benefits of augmented communication, whilst indicating the possible negative impacts of such technology-dependent forms of discourse. In particular, the false dichotomy of online vs offline life is discussed. As such, this book aims to provide a starting point for discussion on this topic as well as highlighting a research agenda.

Keywords Digital communication · Face-to-face interactions · Technology · Language · Applied linguistics · Sociolinguistics

CHAPTER 1

Introduction

Abstract This chapter introduces the topic of augmented communication and sets it in context, providing a brief definition and then explaining the aims and purposes of the book. It also presents the research methodology and an overview of each chapter.

Keywords Digital communication · Face-to-face interactions · Technology · Language · Applied linguistics · Sociolinguistics

It is a truism to say that technology has changed the way we communicate, rather like stating that the earth is still round. It is an observation which is often made and then explained with a few clichéd examples, such as the internet making communication quicker, things being 'a click away' or the coining of new vocabulary like the well-known 'to google' verb. New words have always been coined, but never at the rate they are currently being added (Michel et al. 2011). Some attribute technology's influence to the accelerated pace of these changes whereas others, such as Van Dijk (2012), claim that rather than causing these changes, technology merely amplifies them.

This book looks at the immense changes in human behaviour and the possible impact on society and our minds that advances in information communication technology (ICT) are bringing about *as we speak.* Viewing the issue of online communication vs offline communication as a 'false dichotomy' (Tagg 2015, 81), I examine the way these two

© The Author(s) 2019   1
R. S. Pinner, *Augmented Communication,*
https://doi.org/10.1007/978-3-030-02080-4_1

realms are blurring in face-to-face communication and thus having a profound impact on language and the way we speak to one another in person. One of the phenomena that is most easily observed is *augmented communication*.

Many claims have been levelled at technology destroying face-to-face conversations. One study claims the mere presence of a mobile phone can reduce the quality of conversations and closeness (Przybylski and Weinstein 2013). Another study asserted that, despite their awareness that phones can impair the quality of conversations, 62% of individuals were observed using mobiles in the presence of others (Drago 2015). People find it rude to be ignored in favour of a smartphone, which is why such people who do so are sometimes called *cellfish*. Sherry Turkle, once a great proponent of the digital self, now equates our over-reliance on technology with a withdrawal from personal and meaningful relationships (2012), and even warns that digital devices could lead to a decrease in our capacity for empathy (2015).

Whilst aspects of these arguments are certainly valid, they do not present the whole picture. Although there are bad practices, phones are also used not just to facilitate, but also to enhance face-to-face communication. This book is about the fact that we now often rely on our phones and other networked devices to make conversation, even when we are talking face-to-face with people in real time.

1.1   Brief Definition of Augmented Communication

In its original sense, augmented communication refers to speakers with a disability utilising technology in order to facilitate conversation (American Speech-Language-Hearing Association 2017). World-renowned British physicist Stephen Hawking's voice box is a very clear example of this. When Jean-Dominique Bauby was paralysed after a stroke and could only blink his left eyelid, augmented communication allowed him and his speech therapist to produce the book *The Diving Bell and The Butterfly* (1997).

However, my observations suggest that now augmented communication is adopted by people with ordinary speech as a way to further enhance their face-to-face conversations. Such observations have been made in various parts of the developed world on a daily basis as people communicate in societies with high technological permeation. People do not simply talk about their children or their cats doing something cute, they show a photo of it or even a video on their phones whilst describing the action. Furthermore, it is equally likely that people would be talking about a video featuring a cat that isn't even their own, or some other viral video. The extent of augmented communication is clearly visible when we look around us at how people's talk incorporates networked media.

There are examples of augmented communication in many of the photos on the *Humans of New York* (HONY) photoblog. A post from 16 September 2015 featured a young couple in the background, holding their phone in focus to provide a visual cue for the story they are describing (see Fig. 1.1). As the accompanying story makes clear, the couple show a picture on their phone which captures the moment they first met and interacted. The man talks about how he was so nervous that his body language showed his discomfort, which we can simultaneously see in the picture. In this way, the image provides what I shall refer to as *immediate authenticity*, by heightening the veracity of the story through the addition of visual media, as well as extending on the verbal descriptions. In using this image to augment their conversation with the HONY photographer, Brandon Stanton, the couple in the picture are utilising *exomemory*, which is a repository of stored information that exists outside the mind and yet is accessible to us through digital handheld devices. In the Pixar movie *Inside Out*, during a Skype conversation Meg shows her phone to Riley to describe a new hockey teammate, which is an interesting example of digital to analogue and back to digital (all done through computer graphics). I have observed instances of augmented communication in popular US series such as *Mr. Robot* and *Rick and Morty*. Within the popular media there are frequent examples of phones being used for augmented communication, and countless other cultural examples which suggest the widespread permeation of this phenomenon in developed affluent societies with high smartphone permeation. I have also witnessed augmented communication on Japanese panel shows and Argentinian news, as well as having made ethnographic field observations in Asia, America and Europe.

The most common form of augmented communication is the use of phones to show pictures or other digital media, which I refer to as **multi-modal augmenting**. In this way, people are augmenting their communication and employing ICT to heighten the visual impact or *immediate authenticity* of our conversations. Other examples of augmented communication involve the use of search engines to expand

Humans of New York
17 hrs

"I first met her in church last October. I wanted to talk to her for months but I was too nervous. I'd never gone on a date or had a girlfriend before. All my friends kept helping me think of strategies to ask her out. But I kept saying that I'd do it later. I kept saying that I was too busy with college applications to have a girlfriend. But really I was just too scared. After my applications were finished, I ran out of excuses. So I asked her to sit next to me in church. When the service was over, I walked her to the door and asked her out. My friends were all watching and they snapped this picture. I was crossing my arms because I was so nervous. I'd never had a conversation with a girl for that long."

269k Likes 5.5k Comments 5k Shares

👍 Like   💬 Comment   ➦ Share

Fig. 1.1   From HONY Facebook page 16 September 2015

on existing knowledge, or to make up for a knowledge deficit, which I refer to as **augmented cognition** and which relies upon the use of exomemory. In other cases, augmented communication is used not only to visually enhance and add impact to the conversation, but may also become the talking point itself. An example might be someone showing a new app on his or her phone. This type of augmented communication is referred to as **meta-augmenting**. The final type is when people add others into a conversation, overstepping the geophysical and temporal boundaries of the present face-to-face conversation and blurring online and offline interactions into one. This final type is referred to as **augmented participation**.

With each category of augmented communication, the use of mobile networked digital devices becomes an ad hoc part of discourse, and thus relies on a range of modern day social skills. Lankshear and Knobel (2008) recognise the plurality of such skills, and make a case for digital literacies as an important psychosocial competency or life skill. These new literacies are now an integral part of participatory culture and the heightened power of consumers-as-producers with more influence in determining how things are disseminated, which is referred to as *spreadable media* (Jenkins et al. 2013). Not only do people need to possess a digital communication device and know how to use it (implying a certain level of social capital), they also need to be able to multitask and engage in the conversation whilst simultaneously finding what they need from the device. This could lead to a 'potentially fruitful interplay [between] local face-to-face communication [and] online mediated communication' (Van Dijk 2012, 5). It has been long established that the tools and technologies we adopt have a profound effect on shaping our society, our interactions, and even our very nature as humans (Clark 2003). This makes the possibly widespread practice of augmented communication something of great significance for future research.

1.2   KEY CONCEPTS

The following is a brief literature review and list of key concepts underpinning the analytical framework for this inquiry. As the process of conducting and writing about ethnographies is one which emphasises various levels of analysis, it is not easy or even desirable to demarcate between data and analysis, and thus this book is not structured in the standard way of the literature review, methods, data analysis, etc. Rather, this book presents the study as a narrative of coming to a better understanding of the central phenomenon. As such, data and analysis are presented side-by-side with accompanying references to the literature. This unconventional structure should help shed deeper light on augmented communication in context, but as such it necessitates a somewhat different approach.

1.2.1   Polymedia

Today, there are so many options available to people about how to communicate that is has been suggested that the media selected for the communication also carries its own significance. Thus, the way we send messages also contains additional messages through the medium in which the message is conveyed, and it largely boils down to what our choices say about us, our relationships and the way we communicate. Polymedia is an attempt to describe situations 'in which the media are mediated by the relationship as well as the other way around' (Madianou and Miller 2012a, 148). An illustrative example might be someone choosing to send a text to end a romantic relationship. In choosing to send a text rather than communicating face-to-face, an additional message is conveyed. My personal experience suggests that the receiver might be more offended, will feel less valued and disposed of, but the sender likely chose this method in order to avoid having to deal with the reality in person. Here, the sending of the text and the way the message can be interpreted intermingle with the media. However, polymedia and polymediation are complex theoretical terms, expanded upon since their original coinage by Madianou and Miller (2012a, b) to become an 'umbrella term that describes our modern media landscape' and the way we find ourselves part of that landscape or reality (Dunn 2015, 110). The concept of polymedia goes beyond the notion of *convergence culture* (Jenkins 2006) and attempts to describe the place 'where users have their realities' (Herbig et al. 2015b, xx). An important feature of this is that the notion of polymedia is less technologically deterministic than previous work on the media ecology which posited that technology shapes societies, and emphasises the process and agency of society in also shaping technology and vice versa.

> As a consequence, with polymedia the primary concern shifts from the constraints imposed by each individual medium to an emphasis upon the social, emotional and moral consequences of choosing between those different media. (Madianou and Miller 2012b, 169)

1.2.2 Networked Society

Although this could be taken as being fairly self-evident, the extent of modern societies' overlapping networks is simultaneously mind-boggling in its scope and reach. In his groundbreaking work on the Network Society, Van Dijk (2012) discusses the way networks of electronic information mediate our lives and profoundly shape our experience. Whilst not the focus of this study, it is certainly an important part of the backdrop, as this network is ever with us and ever connecting us, ensuring we are 'always on' (Baron 2008) and necessitating new ways of theorising communication for hyperconnected societies.

1.2.3 Exomemory

In this book, I use the term exomemory to refer to the way networked or digitally stored information can act as a repository to be drawn upon during real-time face-to-face interaction. Exomemory was first coined in Hannu Rahaniemi's 2010 science fiction novel *The Quantum Thief*. This was then developed by Baym (2015), who explained that various online repositories of information can act as a form of 'proto-exomemory' (2015, 26). However, I feel that we can already dispense with the proto-prefix, simply because these technologies do not need to be integrated *under the skin* in order to be a part of us, our thinking and our way of being. This is because of Clark's notion of natural born cyborgs, as explained below (see Sect. 1.2.6). This is also why I discuss augmented cognition as a part of augmented communication, even though the devices we use in everyday life do not (yet) feature neurological interfaces. Although indirectly, this is also linked to the concept of prosthetic memory; the argument that literature, film, and other cultural repositories can potentially expand the experiences of an individual to form a shared memory across cultures, giving access to otherwise unavailable experiences beyond an individual's lifespan or social position (Landsberg 2004).

In order to utilise exomemory, people require a specific set of skills and digital literacies that allow them to select, rely upon and apply in real time the type of information we need when we need it, which is very much tied up with the theory of polymedia. An example would be choosing to use Google Maps to learn about the location of your next destination, and using online reviews to help choose a restaurant.

Although not specifically exo- in itself, this type of knowledge is how we come to rely on other forms of externally stored information. Thus, these literacies are the reason for our increasing reliance on networked or digitally stored information, and they *depend* on our *dependence* on technology to go about our lives in this manner.

1.2.4   Immediate Authenticity

This is my own term, and the concept refers to the way that certain forms of media, such as visuals and other networked information, can bring people closer to the main points of a conversation through multimodal input. In other words, if I talk about a topic hitherto unknown to my friend, this may have little impact or seem rather unfamiliar at first, whereas if I introduce the new topic and show pictures, videos or other type of information this adds to the impact and creates immediate authenticity, through enabling a deeper level of engagement by making the topic more real and more present via multimodal input. This is much the same as if the topic of conversation was actually visible, a famous example being Steve Jobs' demonstrating how his new laptop can fit into an envelope. This term does not specifically relate only to digital applications, but anything talked about which has an immediate visual.

1.2.5   Transportable Identities

Identity is an important aspect of this study, and naturally I take a multifaceted view of identity and see it as both dynamic, fluid and fractal (Seargeant and Tagg 2014; Vincent and Fortunati 2014; Lin 2013). One useful theory for understanding our choices when enacting various parts of our identities comes from Zimmerman (1998), who differentiates three identities which speakers invoke during discourse.

- Situated identities: explicitly conferred by the context of communication, as with doctor/patient identities in the context of a health clinic or teacher/student identities in the context of a classroom.
- Discourse identities: as participants orient themselves to particular discourse roles in the unfolding organisation of the interaction (e.g. initiator, listener and questioner).

- Transportable identities, which are latent or implicit but can be invoked during the interaction, such as when a teacher alludes to her identity as a mother or as a keen gardener during a language lesson (see also Ushioda 2011, Richards 2006).

When people interact in different social contexts, they might often invoke transportable identities as a way of showing that they are not merely the sum of their situational identity. This is something which has relevance for augmented communication as through blended online and offline interactions and identities, we are likely to invoke transportable identities, and this may even at times be done unwittingly (Pinner 2016). This has clear overlaps and with another phenomenon known as context collapse; the process by which sharing digital content produces a myriad of new contexts in which the original content is shared and viewed by others (Marwick and boyd 2011).

1.2.6   *Extended Mind (Natural Born Cyborgs)*

The theory of extended mind, much like the idea of polymedia, views cognition as a dynamic process that influences and is influenced by our interactions with external reality. It considers not just how the body influences the mind but also how the mind influences the body. This idea has been extended upon famously by Logic and Metaphysics professor Andy Clark (2001, 2003) who discusses our reliance on technology (and historically tools in general) to extend our human experiences beyond the realms of our own bodies and minds. Clark argues that we are natural born cyborgs, and that although exterior to us, the technological tools that we employ are intrinsic to our experience of the world. For this reason, I do not feel I am misusing terms I later apply to this inquiry, such as augmented cognition or exomemory.

1.3   AIMS AND PURPOSE OF THE BOOK

The aims of this book are to open up discussion on this new phenomenon and propose a research agenda. Both positive and negative aspects of augmented communication will be discussed, but it is my intention that serious consideration be paid to this development as it could have major ramifications for how discourse is conducted.

The primary research questions that motivated this project were:

- If we are using augmented communication as part of everyday face-to-face interactions, what are the different types of augmented communication and what are the primary functions of doing so?
- How does augmented communication alter conversations? What does it add to a conversation that cannot be achieved without a networked digital device?
- How does the act of augmenting work in practice?

I posit augmented communication to be an automatic linguistic consequence of our polymediated age (Herbig et al. 2015a). Of course, another aspect of the study was my reading of the literature, especially searching for relevant studies into the language of social media, digital-and computer-mediated communication. These discussions further implicated more sociological issues, such as polymedia, convergence culture, transmedia and the networked society.

1.4   METHODOLOGY: AUTOETHNOGRAPHY
AND OBSERVATION DATA

This section offers an explanation of the data-collection techniques and locations, as well as a brief statement about narratives and the analytical approaches utilised in order to gain meaning from social interactions in context, particularly focusing on social networks, looking at how individual relationships and social ties to communities are affected and played out through real-time face-to-face interactions. Emphasis is also placed on identity, in particular the fractal and multiple nature of identity as it emerges in different contexts with different speakers.

This book presents initial findings from ongoing research utilising autoethnographic data to provide evidence-based observations for the phenomena of augmented communication. Ethnography involves the researcher being immersed in the everyday life of the social group(s) under observation. In this way, '[t]he task of the fieldworker is to enter into the matrix of meanings of the researched, to participate in their system of organized activities' (Wax 1980, 272–73). As my earliest observations arose naturally by simply being with my existing friends and colleagues (an indicator of the already high permeation of augmented communication), I did not need to seek out any particular groups or to attempt to become one of them, or even to make any major changes in my own life. The field of my research came to me, in this way. For this reason, this is autoethnographic research, where the author/researcher attempts to 'systematically analyse [...] personal experience' (Ellis et al. 2011, 273).

Critics of autoethnography may try to claim it is 'nonanalytic, self-indulgent, irreverent, sentimental, and romantic' (Denzin 2014, 69), but although it does place the researcher/author at the centre of the inquiry they are not the sole agent of the unfurling narrative (Chang 2008). In this way, most of the data I present is ethnographic in origin, yet as the observations and fieldwork were carried out by merely living and engaging as myself, there is an element also of autoethnography which should not be ignored. In this way, the study has collected data from those consenting individuals around me who I met through the normal course of my life. This of course, means that the observations mainly come from people of similar social, cultural and professional background to me. This is a limitation, and hence broader generalisations are to be avoided or applied carefully with the relevant proviso, as is often the case with ethnography and qualitative research more generally. However, I would further qualify this statement by announcing that augmented communication is something I have observed on a very large-scale throughout my travels to developed countries in various continents, something that I see *everyday* as I look around me at how strangers are talking. This is not just here in Japan where I live, but at airports, cafes and on television. The sheer scale of the number of observations I made were initially one of the main problems I faced in refining the design of this study. So, on the one hand, as an ethnographic study I should avoid making broad generalisations, and yet on the other the phenomena I describe seems to be very much permeating developed societies with high smartphone diffusion quite rapidly.

Whilst ethnography has an established place in research into linguistics and sociology, it has recently seen developments as the method is further adapted and developed for collecting data online. For instance, Kozinets (2015) has coined the term *netnography* to describe how internet ethnography is qualitatively different from ordinary ethnography, particularly due to online-specific issues such as access, archiving and ethics. Questions about anonymity when quoted posts are public and easily searchable, the nature of timestamps and the permanence of many online interactions are foregrounded in netnography (Kozinets 2015, 72–77). For Pink et al. (2016), *digital ethnography* is an expansion of ethnography, an adapted form which is still guided by the principles of ethnography and yet with its own adapted principles for the online nature of the work.

Hine (2015, 45) reminds us that 'we access the Internet as embodied social beings', and this is of course extremely prevalent in the present study, as I am working with face-to-face interactions which often take place both online and offline. There is a tendency to feel we are ephemeral when we go online, that we somehow leave our bodies behind and come back to them again when we come back offline. This, of course, is not true. When we are online we are still present in the physical world, albeit with our attention perhaps impaired by the work we are doing on the screen.

Therefore, such an approach made the most intuitive sense as a researcher looking to gain insights into the phenomenon of augmented communication, as it evolves from something mainly associated with speech impairments into something used by people with unimpaired speech as a way of enhancing face-to-face conversations so as to include all the trappings of modern society, with both online and offline aspects merging in real time.

In ethnographic research, the method is inductive and 'evolves in design through the study' (Pink et al. 2016, 3), taking into account the inevitable 'difficulties and dead ends that we all experience' (Silverman 2013, 306). Because, as I mentioned earlier, the study came *to* me as I merely observed changes in conversation patterns that were happening around me with my existing friends and colleagues, the development of my note taking was perhaps the most complex and problematic aspect of the study. As this study grew in scope, I realised that I would need more data and began to take field notes regularly, sometimes during the interactions and conversations. This led to my having logged hundreds of instances of augmented communication over the five years or so which spanned from my initial observations to the current writing up. These were not only with friends, but also observing strangers on trains, at restaurants and airports and even people on television. As a result of the sheer scale of augmented communication, making notes on everything quickly became impossible. Many of my initial notes were partial, and I could only capture a fragment of what was happening, and generally after the first instance, many others would occur but due to the number of instances it was not always practical to continue to log these. This became especially true once I had enough evidence to begin telling people that I was planning to write a study about augmented communication. With my close friends especially, but also with people I had just met, I would find myself often explaining the phenomenon and asking them to reflect on it as part of the conversation. In this way, the conversations became an ad hoc interview of sorts. Although these were not recorded, I logged the main gist and some direct quotes as field notes, which were then later expanded in more detail into a journal. The journal was begun on the 31 of October 2014, but already by this point I had two years of fragmented field notes to collate. Often, I found that looking at the field notes was not enough to fully retrieve and log the observation in the journal, and thus I often needed to look back at my schedule from the time to find out more clearly who I was with, where we had gone and also the other broader context(s) of the original note. In this way, I often had to use a kind of stimulated recall on myself, and whenever practical I would also speak to those I had originally been talking with for further expansion. Field notes should focus on *what* is happening and *how* it happens, rather than trying to expand upon *why* (Emerson et al. 2011).

A further aspect was that in June 2015 I contacted my two sisters and a close friend (all living in England) to ask if they would be able to help my study by sharing their own observations. I gave them very brief instructions about how to conduct systematic self-observation (Rodriguez and Ryave 2002). Their insights were also useful for me, and then later I began working with groups of my own students in Tokyo who were part of my linguistics seminar, which I did for three semesters from autumn 2016 to autumn 2017. With the students, I was especially cautious of any ethical concerns that might arise, and so I made it clear that they could opt out of providing any data by merely claiming to have 'forgotten' or not to have noticed anything. The research task was unassessed and, as much as possible, I felt that the observations were given willingly and with informed consent.

Although I asked these people to help me by conducting systematic self-observation for a period of one week, generally these only resulted in one or two observations of a single occurrence. However, these then provided further entries and confirmed general patterns already observed by the author. The four types of augmented communication use were then identified from these reports. These main categories which arose from the data and observations then form the structure of the centre (Chapters 3 and 4) of this book, as I will outline in the next Sect. (1.4).

Towards the latter part of the study, I had begun taking photographs of augmented communication. Not only my own photographs, but also screenshots from the internet and from films and other programmes that I was watching. In this way, the dataset includes field notes, journal logs, pictures taken by myself and images collected from other sources, as well as data from ad hoc interviews that arose as I explained my research after encountering augmented communication occurring naturally with my fellow interlocutors. All of these data types were used to inform the final analysis as presented here in this book.

1.4.1   The Evolution of the Design in Context

One of my earliest recorded observation of augmented communication, took place in November 2014 when I was out having dinner with two friends in Tokyo (both are Japanese men in their early 40s, one is single and the other married with two children). We were talking about a mutual acquaintance who we hadn't seen for a long time named Chiyori-san, who we had all met when she was a *Maiko* (apprentice Geisha) working in Tokyo. None of us knew Chiyori-san well, and we had met her in 2004 with very little contact since then, but we all felt lucky to know someone like her (i.e. a Geisha, as they are revered in Japanese culture) and had been keen to stay in touch. I looked down at my friend's phone as he proceeded to google her there and then, and we found out what she was up to and were interested to see that she had quit being a Geisha and started up her own organic food company. Without a phone and an internet connection, this conversation would have been a familiar case of merely wondering what someone with whom we have lost contact is now doing. The ability to check in real time as part of the conversation makes this augmented communication, and it greatly alters the pattern of conversation. In drawing on networked resources ad hoc during face-to-face interaction, we draw on forms of *exomemory* (networked or digitally stored information) and the skills and literacies for finding information as we need it, a theme which I develop throughout the book.

In other words, the technology is used to enhance the immediate conversation in real time. The conversation would have ended with 'I don't know what Chiyori-san is doing, haven't seen her in years… I wonder what she is doing'. However, thanks to mobile internet and advances in ICT (as well as the fact that Chiyori-san had a website and an online digital shadow) we were able to find out exactly what she was doing and what she now looked like. This example of augmented communication shows the use of search engines to expand on existing knowledge, or to make up for a knowledge deficit, which could be argued as a form of augmented cognition. One of the friends has a very good command of English, but the other is still learning and so, combined with my Japanese competence, I noticed that we often used our phones to help us talk. However, I quickly realised that conversations which were reliant on digital technology were not limited to situations where there is a linguistic barrier. Indeed, I quickly observed other people using their phones as part of a conversation, even when they shared the same first language.

I began to refer to this as augmented communication because I intuitively felt this described the practices I was observing. I began making journal entries whenever I could, but even this quickly became too large a task. During a single night, I might observe tens of instances where someone would show me their phone as part of the conversation, and I realised it would be impossible to document all of them, especially over a long period. I attempted to observe how people use their phones in cafes, a similar method to that employed by Zeitlyn (2009), however, this method did not yield rich enough data for me to know *how* people were using their phones within the conversations, and what types of augmented communication were being used. Instead, I began collecting field notes that recorded the different ways people used their phones, the context and the types of stories people were telling me. I also began to talk to people about augmented communication, often explaining to them that I was planning to write a research paper or monograph about the phenomenon. Again, I made notes and collected records of what people said to me about their own phone usage. In order to complete the study, I analysed and coded the instances, trying to narrow them in such a way as to identify the main categories of augmented communication. These are multimodal augmenting, meta-augmenting, augmented cognition and augmented participation, as mentioned earlier.

This research has also been about me as much as it has been about the people I have talked to and observed, and thus this study involves autoethnographic observations as well, as I reflect on the way I use my phone during face-to-face communication. As usual with an ethnographic inquiry, I am particularly concerned with the implications for society that augmented communication may have, and I have tried to include concerns about any possible divisions, about people being disadvantaged by augmented communication, and to retain a critical perspective through reflection and further inquiry, particularly with my engagement with the relevant research literature.

In this way, the data I will draw on and present for this book comes from my own individual context as a person. I do not present insights from any particular or specific contexts other than my own. Despite this, the potentially widespread nature of augmented communication in developed middle-class societies with high technology penetration seems everywhere hinted at and easily observable, as evidenced by other observations that I have made in the media. This is certainly an area in need of further and larger-scale inquiry.

A final comment needs to be made about those people who have provided me with my observations and data. Many of them are people close to me or whom I have met, and hence, there is an ethical question about using data collected in this way. Therefore, whenever I talked to people at length about augmented communication, I made it clear that I was approaching this subject as a researcher. When I present a story or specific piece of information that could potentially identify one of the people with whom I have interacted, I have either made certain changes in order to protect that person's anonymity, or I have contacted them directly in order to give them the choice to further reflect (participant validation) and allow them to either be an anonymous participant, or if they prefer to be identified and include their own voice, or to ask if they would prefer to be omitted. Whilst my data contains many observations from people who did not know they were being observed, this book contains only data from willing participants who have been consulted and involved in the writing process.

1.5   OVERVIEW

This book is about the way mobile networked digital devices affect face-to-face conversations in ways (both positive and negative) that would not be possible without them. Specifically, I examine how people use smartphones during conversations in order to augment them by applying a range of different communicative strategies. As cognition, memory and language are closely related during the parsing of speech, I inevitably turn to these arguments throughout the book. The structure of this book is informed by the data-driven and inductive approach to the research that I took. As such, data and analysis are not presented separately, but as part of an entwined narrative that makes reference throughout to the existing research literature. In order to make the book more navigable, I intentionally use signposting throughout the book in order to link strands of thought together in a cohesive way. In this way, the book features much forward and backward signposting, which is intentional so as to guide the reader and encourage different, less linear ways of engaging with this book.

In Chapter 2, the historical development of augmented communication in disability is briefly examined. This is in order to show that augmented communication is not a new phenomenon, and has a history of empowerment behind it. Rather than promoting inequality and widening the digital divide, augmented communication was originally developed as a means of giving people a voice and helping to level the playing field of communication. It is hoped that this evaluation will allow for a return to this ideology, and that augmented communication be seen as a potentially empowering phenomena, especially with regard to shifting the power of information away from mainstream media providers.

As mentioned, the central structure of this book is based around the main categories of augmented communication that arose from the data analysis. Chapter 3 will provide examples of augmented communication, in particular by presenting four vignettes of augmented communication in use. These are ethnographic observations, and will be presented with the accompanying level of context and analysis befitting such data. Each vignette provides an example in-use for each of the subsequent types of augmented communication, presented in Chapter 4. These four types are multimodal augmentation, meta-augmenting, augmented cognition and finally augmented participation. In this way, Chapters 3 and 4 mirror each other in structure.

Chapter 5 then takes a step back to provide an analysis and discussion of the issues that surface throughout the presentation of the main types of augmented communication. In particular, issues about attention, the quality of communication, the loss of empathy and other social skills acquired through ordinary face-to-face interactions. Although I pay heed to these warnings, I also point out that such claims are still in need of further research. I discuss alternative perspectives on these 'problems', viewing them rather as 'changes'. The arguments levelled against, say, the negative impact of technology on attention and memory for example, are not new and have been made about all new technologies, from the creation of written systems for preserving language, the invention of the printing press, right up to the invention of the telephone and television. It is true that these technologies have altered the structure of our brains and our society, but these changes are inevitable consequences of our development as a technology-utilising species.

In particular, I develop the concept of *exomemory* in order to address the arguments about how these technologies affect our minds and our conversations. This will be developed more fully in Sect. 4.3 when I discuss augmented cognition as an aspect of augmented communication, although these are mentioned throughout the book.

In Chapter 6, I provide an overall conclusion and discuss the way that augmented communication may be further researched in the future. I also once again try to highlight my role as an applied linguist carrying out an autoethnographic inquiry, and thus I acknowledge my own position in the research. In doing so, I attempt to avoid essentialising the debate about smartphones and other networked mobile technologies by taking 'sides' or concurring one way or the other as to whether their influence is positive or negative. More realistically, the picture is double-sided. This book merely presents my observations and analysis from my own point of view, advocating a critical stance which accepts the changes undergoing our communicative practices and wonders as to the possible implications that they bring.

References

American Speech-Language-Hearing Association. 2017. "Augmentative and Alternative Communication (AAC)." Accessed February 17, 2017. http://www.asha.org/public/speech/disorders/AAC/.

Baron, Naomi S. 2008. *Always on: Language in an Online and Mobile World.* Oxford: Oxford University Press.

Baym, Nancy K. 2015. *Personal Connections in the Digital Age, Digital Media and Socitey.* Cambridge, UK: Polity Press.

Chang, Heewon. 2008. *Autoethnography as Method.* London: Routledge.

Clark, Andy. 2001. "Natural-Born Cyborgs?" In *Cognitive Technology: Instruments of Mind*, edited by Meurig Beynon, Chrystopher L. Nehaniv, and Kerstin Dautenhahn, 17–24. London: Springer.

Clark, Andy. 2003. *Natural-Born Cyborgs: Minds, Technologies, and the Future of Human Intelligence.* New York: Oxford University Press.

Denzin, Norman K. 2014. "Interpretive Autoethnography." In *Qualitative Research Methods*, edited by Helen Salmon, 2nd ed, vol. 17. London: Sage.

Drago, Emily. 2015. "The Effect of Technology on Face-to-Face Communication." *The Elon Journal of Undergraduate Research in Communications* 6 (1): 13–19.

Dunn, Robert Andrew. 2015. "Polyreality." In *Beyond New Media: Discourse and Critique in a Polymediated Age*, edited by Art Herbig, Andrew F. Herrmann, and Adam W. Tyma, 109–24. London: Lexington Books.

Ellis, Carolyn, Tony E. Adams, and Arthur P. Bochner. 2011. "Autoethnography: An Overview." *Historical Social Research/Historische Sozialforschung* 36 (4): 273–90.

Emerson, Robert M., Rachel I. Fretz, and Linda L. Shaw. 2011. *Writing Ethnographic Fieldnotes*, 2nd ed. Chicago, IL: University of Chicago Press.

Herbig, Art, Andrew F. Herrmann, and Adam W. Tyma (eds.). 2015a. *Beyond New Media: Discourse and Critique in a Polymediated Age*. London: Lexington Books.

Herbig, Art, Andrew F. Herrmann, and Adam W. Tyma. 2015b. "Introduction: The Beginnings #WeNeedaWord." In *Beyond New Media: Discourse and Critique in a Polymediated Age*, edited by Art Herbig, Andrew F. Herrmann, and Adam W. Tyma, ix–xxiv. London: Lexington Books.

Hine, Christine. 2015. *Ethnography for the Internet: Embedded, Embodied and Everyday*. London: Bloomsbury.

Jenkins, Henry. 2006. *Convergence Culture: Where Old and New Media Collide*. New York, NY: New York University Press.

Jenkins, Henry, Sam Ford, and Joshua Green. 2013. *Spreadable Media: Creating Value and Meaning in a Networked Culture*. New York, NY: New York University Press.

Kozinets, Robert V. 2015. *Netnography: Redefined*, 2nd ed. London: Sage.

Landsberg, Alison. 2004. *Prosthetic Memory: The Transformation of American Remembrance in the Age of Mass Culture*. Chichester, NY: Columbia University Press.

Lankshear, Colin, and Michael Knobel (eds.). 2008. *Digital Literacies: Concepts, Policies and Practices*. New York: Peter Lang.

Lin, Angel (ed.). 2013. *Problematizing Identity: Everyday Struggles in Language, Culture, and Education*. London: Routledge.

Madianou, Mirca, and Daniel Miller. 2012a. *New Media and Migration: Transnational Families and Polymedia*. London: Routledge.

Madianou, Mirca, and Daniel Miller. 2012b. "Polymedia: Towards a New Theory of Digital Media in Interpersonal Communication." *International Journal of Cultural Studies* 16 (2): 169–87. https://doi.org/10.1177/1367877912452486.

Marwick, Alice E., and danah boyd. 2011. "I Tweet Honestly, I Tweet Passionately: Twitter Users, Context Collapse, and the Imagined Audience." *New Media & Society* 13 (1): 114–33. https://doi.org/10.1177/1461444810365313.

Michel, Jean-Baptiste, Yuan Kui Shen, Aviva Presser Aiden, Adrian Veres, Matthew K. Gray, Joseph P. Pickett, Dale Hoiberg, Dan Clancy, Peter Norvig,

Jon Orwant, Steven Pinker, Martin A. Nowak, and Erez Lieberman Aiden. 2011. "Quantitative Analysis of Culture Using Millions of Digitized Books." *Science* 331 (6014): 176–82. https://doi.org/10.1126/science.1199644.

Pink, Sarah, Heather Horst, John Postill, Larissa Hjorth, Tania Lewis, and Jo Tacchi. 2016. *Digital Ethnography: Principles and Practice*. London: Springer.

Pinner, Richard Stephen. 2016. "Constructing and Managing Transportable Identities on Social Networking Sites." *Explorations in Teacher Education* 23 (2): 2–5.

Przybylski, Andrew K, and Netta Weinstein. 2013. "Can You Connect with Me Now? How the Presence of Mobile Communication Technology Influences Face-to-Face Conversation Quality." *Journal of Social and Personal Relationships* 30 (3): 237–46.

Richards, Keith. 2006. "'Being the Teacher': Identity and Classroom Conversation." *Applied Linguistics* 27 (1): 51–77.

Rodriguez, Noelie M, and Alan Ryave. 2002. *Systematic Self-Observation: A Method for Researching the Hidden and Elusive Features of Everyday Social Life*, vol. 49. London: Sage.

Seargeant, Philip, and Caroline Tagg (eds.). 2014. *The Language of Social Media: Identity and Community on the Internet*. Basingstoke: Palgrave Macmillan.

Silverman, David. 2013. *Doing Qualitative Research: A Practical Handbook*. London: Sage.

Tagg, Caroline. 2015. *Exploring Digital Communication: Language in Action*. London: Routledge.

Turkle, Sherry. 2012. *Alone Together: Why We Expect More from Technology and Less from Each Other*. Philadelphia, PA: Basic books.

Turkle, Sherry. 2015. *Reclaiming Conversation: The Power of Talk in a Digital Age*. New York: Penguin Press.

Ushioda, Ema. 2011. "Motivating Learners to Speak as Themselves." In *Identity, Motivation and Autonomy in Language Learning*, edited by Garold Murray, Xuesong Gao, and Terry E. Lamb, 11–25. Bristol: Multilingual Matters.

Van Dijk, Jan. 2012. *The Network Society*, 3rd ed. London: Sage.

Vincent, Jane, and Leopoldina Fortunati. 2014. "The Emotional Identity of the Mobile Phone." In *The Routledge Companion to Mobile Media*, edited by Gerard Goggin and Larissa Hjorth, 312–19. London: Routledge.

Wax, Murray L. 1980. "Paradoxes of 'Consent' to the Practice of Fieldwork." *Social Problems* 27 (3): 272–83. https://doi.org/10.2307/800246.

Zeitlyn, David. 2009. *Digital Anthropology Report*. Kent: University of Kent.

Zimmerman, Don H. 1998. "Identity, Context and Interaction." In *Identities in Talk*, edited by C. Antaki and S. Widdicombe, 87–106. London: Sage.

CHAPTER 2

History of Augmented Communication: Technology and Disability

Abstract This chapter presents a short overview of augmented communication as a way of helping those with speech disabilities to communicate. Certain works of historical importance are discussed, such as *The Diving Bell and The Butterfly*.

Keywords Disability · Face-to-face interactions · Technology · Language · Applied linguistics · Sociolinguistics · Augmentative and Alternative Communication

Augmented communication is already a recognised phenomenon, although it is usually known as Augmentative and Alternative Communication (AAC), which describes how technology can be utilised to help hearing and speech impaired people communicate more easily and convey their messages with greater accuracy. Communication is facilitated using tools of varying degrees of complexity, from those as simple as a board with the alphabet on to spell out words, to advanced computer systems which use prediction and have their own voice.

© The Author(s) 2019   21
R. S. Pinner, *Augmented Communication*,
https://doi.org/10.1007/978-3-030-02080-4_2

2.1   HISTORICAL USES OF THE TERM AUGMENTATIVE
AND ALTERNATIVE COMMUNICATION

When Jean-Dominique Bauby, the journalist and editor of *Elle* magazine, was paralysed after a stroke in 1995, he was left with only the ability to blink his left eyelid. With the help of his speech therapist Claude Mendibil (and their shared patience and motivation) the novel *The Diving Bell and The Butterfly* was written using a process called partner-assisted scanning in which one person scans over the alphabet until the other indicates where to stop. Despite losing his voice after his tracheotomy in 1985, Professor Stephen Hawking[1] is still able to give lectures thanks to augmented communication. When my step-father lost the capacity to speak coherently after a brain operation, my mum created a book of photos and high-frequency symbols which we used in order to facilitate conversations. In these ways, technology has been enabling those for whom language might be lost to remain in contact with society and to contribute as equals. Because language is perhaps one of the greatest tools at our disposal for constructing our identities, the importance of this work is hard to deny.

AAC has several categories, including Unaided and Aided, the latter of which can be defined as either high or low tech (Beukelman and Miranda 2013). Special significance is generally given to technologies that can facilitate speech (Hemsley and Balandin 2017), which will be discussed in the following section. However, it is worth noting also that unaided forms of AAC include facial expressions, gestures and sign-languages. Clearly, AAC is a broad area which encompasses many different types of assistive methods for providing a diverse range of people with better facilities for speech.

Also in 1985 (the same year as Hawking's tracheotomy), a new journal named *Augmentative and Alternative Communication* was launched in order to provide a forum for research and innovation in helping people with speech disabilities to find a voice. The journal was associated with *The International Society for Augmentative and Alternative Communication*, which holds an annual conference and seeks to further the development of solutions for speech impaired individuals. One key role of this work is to investigate, implement and facilitate the creation of new technologies that enable people to talk or communicate.

2.2   THE ROLE OF TECHNOLOGY IN HELPING PEOPLE TO SPEAK

AAC does not necessarily require modern technology or high-end computers to be effective, although this is clearly an important aspect of it. Recently, there has been a sharp increase in the number of children being diagnosed on the autistic spectrum (King and Bearman 2009). AAC has been applied successfully in ways which enable children with autism to participate more evenly in educational settings. Assistive technologies have also been used to help dyslexic children learn to read, and indeed the applications for educational technology in general aim to personalise each users' experience and provide a fine-tuned educational experience to accommodate the wide spectrum of learners' needs in modern institutional settings.

A well-known example of an AAC device widely in use is the GoTalk, manufactured by the Attainment Company, which was set up in 1979 to provide technological AAC solutions for all ages and a range of disabilities. There are several models, but the GoTalk essentially works by recording a spoken message which is then assigned to a button with a symbol. These can be customised for the individual, who can then simply press the button for high-frequency utterances that she or he may need throughout the day.

Of course, perhaps the most recognisable example of AAC is the software and hardware that allows Professor Stephen Hawking to communicate. A video on YouTube entitled *Stephen Hawking—How Is He Talking?*[2] Has reached over 900,000 views since it was uploaded in 2014, and a more updated video created by Bloomberg in 2015 based on the recent upgrades facilitated by Intel has already reached over half a million views.[3] There is a fascination with Hawking, not just because of his theories and his intellect, but as a survivor of motor neurone disease and a champion of AAC. Although his voice is made from a 1980s voice synthesiser, now archaic in comparison to newer versions of the technology, Hawking considers the voice a part of his identity. Although he has been offered newer versions, he prefers to keep the original one. According to an article in the tech magazine *WIRED*:

> Hawking is very attached to his voice: in 1988, when Speech Plus gave him the new synthesizer, the voice was different so he asked them to replace it with the original. His voice had been created in the early '80s by MIT engineer Dennis Klatt, a pioneer of text-to-speech algorithms. (Medeiros 2015)

Hawking's case is an excellent example of how technology has given a voice to someone who otherwise would have been suffering from locked-in syndrome; trapped inside his body without any means of expressing himself. At the time of writing, Hawking uses one muscle in his cheek to deliver lectures, write papers and books, browse the internet, keep up with his correspondence and hold daily conversations. Playing on the lighthearted jokes about his outdated computer voice, in 2017 for UK charity Comic Relief, a video was made of famous actors and comedians auditioning to become the new voice of Stephen Hawking.[4]

However, AAC is quite distinct from the version of *augmented communication* which I describe in this book, with the main difference being that AAC is primarily concerned with giving voice to those individuals who otherwise would find expression through language difficult. Such people range from children with autism to elderly people with Alzheimer's. Speech impairments can originate physiologically, neurologically and even psychologically, and some are present at birth, acquired through disease or injury, and others may simply develop from other myriad factors. Despite this focus on helping the speech impaired, there are broader definitions, such the one below which comes from the *International Society for Augmentative and Alternative Communication's* website:

> AAC is a set of tools and strategies that an individual uses to solve everyday *communicative challenges*. Communication can take many forms such as: speech, a shared glance, text, gestures, facial expressions, touch, sign language, symbols, pictures, speech-generating devices, etc. Everyone uses multiple forms of communication, based upon the context and our communication partner. Effective communication occurs when the intent and meaning of one individual is understood by another person. *The form is less important than the successful understanding of the message.* (Burkhart 2011, emphasis added)

Clearly, the above definition encompasses non-verbal behaviours which are a naturally occurring part of face-to-face communication, but the distinguishing features are overcoming challenges (presumably those faced by individuals with any kind of speech impairment), and understanding being more important than the form in which the message is conveyed. I posit these to be the main differences between AAC and augmented communication as it is used in this book. With augmented communication, the added use of technology is the focus, with interpretation and meaning being of secondary importance to the mode. This is because, in this book, I am focusing on the utilisation of high-tech, networked tools (primarily, but not exclusively, smartphones), in order to add something to the conversation which could not be achieved otherwise. I am looking at how smartphones and mobile networked devices are *changing* conversations that are had face-to-face, and the way these devices are used, not to overcome challenges, but to augment conversations in ways which are media-centred and rely on outside informational repositories and connectivity that expand beyond the immediate interaction.

2.3 SUMMARY

This chapter has presented the historical background, showing that augmented communication is not new, but that it has traditionally been used to support those for whom speech is difficult or restricted.

Clearly, although the term augmented communication has traditionally been associated with speech impairment through the work on AAC, this book is about a very different type of augmented communication. It is not my intention to detract from this excellent work by labelling the phenomena of using digital devices in face-to-face communication as *augmented communication* when this term is already in use to describe techniques and systems employed to help those unfortunate enough to have their speech impaired. I would like to make it known here that I applaud the work being done by those researching AAC, and I have a great deal of empathy for those individuals who suffer from speech impairment. In the very first issue of the journal of *Augmentative and Alternative Communication*, the editor David Yoder opened his editorial with the following quote from educational consultant Rick Creech:

> I know of no other handicap as great, or having as great an effect on a person's psychological and sociological development, as being unable to speak. (cited in Yoder 1985, 1)

With this I am in complete agreement, especially as an applied linguist myself. The work on AAC has given a voice to those who otherwise would not be heard. They range from famous authors such as Dominique Bauby (locked-in syndrome) and brilliant scientists such as

Stephen Hawking (amyotrophic lateral sclerosis), to elderly people suffering from dementia, people with autism, those with aphasia and dyspraxia, as well as individuals with intellectual impairments or brain damage. Whilst this book now moves away from such individuals, I feel that this chapter is vital in setting the stage for the newer phenomena being described.

Augmented communication as utilised by those who need assistance to speak is generally much slower than the rate of normal verbal communication. However, what happens when people who do not have speech impairments utilise augmented communication techniques to enhance their face-to-face conversations? Before I discuss this, let us take a look at how augmented communication appears in everyday life in countries where many people now carry smartphones and other networked devices in their pockets.

2.3.1   Reflection

Readers are invited to consider the central role of language to our identity and social interactions, and the powerlessness we might experience when we are unable to communicate normally.

There are only a few times in my life when I have completely lost the power of my voice. The most recent time was in 2015 when I caught laryngitis. It was utterly debilitating. I remember Kimie, my wife, brought me a cup of tea whilst I was working at the computer. I was so grateful for the tea, but I could only express thanks using my eyes, unless I wrote it on the notepad which I had to take with me everywhere. I felt not using my voice robbed me of my identity. The importance of language in constructing our identities and forming social bonds cannot be overstated, and indeed it is common to remark that language is one of the most defining aspects of what it is to be human. If the way we communicate changes due to technology, does that imply that our humanity is coming to depend more on the technological tools at our disposal? The rest of this book will examine this question in more detail.

Notes

1. Sadly, Professor Hawking died shortly after the writing of this book. I opted to retain the present tense for the description of him.
2. The video is available at https://youtu.be/UErbwiJH1dI.

3. The video is available at https://youtu.be/OTmPw4iy0hk.
4. The video, entitled *Stephen Hawking's New Voice | Comic Relief Originals* can be watched at https://youtu.be/PqXOlfwlVag and has already received over 3 million views.

REFERENCES

Beukelman, David, and Pat Mirenda (eds.). 2013. *Augmentative and Alternative Communication: Supporting Children and Adults with Complex Communication Needs*, 4th ed. Maryland, BA: Paul Brookes.
Burkhart, Linda J. 2011. "What Is AAC?" Accessed October 14. https://www.isaac-online.org/english/what-is-aac/.
Hemsley, Bronwyn, and Susan Balandin. 2017. "Evidence and Innovation in AAC Research: Expanding Borders and Boundaries for a Global Audience." *Augmentative and Alternative Communication* 33 (1): 1–2. https://doi.org/10.1080/07434618.2017.1280082.
King, Marissa, and Peter Bearman. 2009. "Diagnostic Change and the Increased Prevalence of Autism." *International Journal of Epidemiology* 38 (5): 1224–34. https://doi.org/10.1093/ije/dyp261.
Medeiros, Joao. 2015. "How Intel Gave Stephen Hawking a Voice." *WIRED*.
Yoder, David. 1985. "Editorial." *Augmentative and Alternative Communication* 1 (1): 1. https://doi.org/10.1080/07434618512331273451.

CHAPTER 3

Augmented Communication as a Modern Phenomenon in Ordinary Speech

Abstract Augmented communication is presented as it relates to people with normal speech who utilise digital devices naturally as part of their face-to-face conversations. Special attention is placed on context, identity and community by highlighting narrative samples from the data in the form of vignettes, each of which is designed to introduce one of the four types of augmented communication.

Keywords Digital communication · Face-to-face interactions · Technology · Language · Applied linguistics · Sociolinguistics

The following excerpt from the Canadian online magazine *University Affairs* shows quite clearly how augmented communication takes place in real time, and blurs the boundary between the false dichotomy of online and offline.

> I have my office hours on Friday afternoons. [...]
> Recently, I have been hearing an echo in the room. A detailed answer or explanation that I give to one student will be delivered back to me with further questions an hour later by another student who wasn't even in the room for the initial explanation. How have my seemingly private responses spread so quickly? [...]

© The Author(s) 2019
R. S. Pinner, *Augmented Communication*,
https://doi.org/10.1007/978-3-030-02080-4_3

I have come to discover that my office hours are being tweeted, Facebooked and blogged about in real time. The self-effacing student sitting on the couch beside my desk is not typing notes – she is posting live updates to a Facebook group dedicated to my course. And the compelling question she asks, which appears to have been stimulated from our constructive discussions, was actually text-messaged to her by another student who is in Toronto for the weekend.

These online activities by my students can sometimes feel like espionage, but they can also be helpful. By posting my replies to Facebook or Twitter, the students are saving me from having to explain the same concepts over and over again. And by relaying questions from students who are away, they are helping me to connect with the entire class. But, if I give a less-than-eloquent reply or inadvertently provide one too many details about the exam, my answers can be broadcast to hundreds of pupils and can come back to haunt me. (Smith 2017)

In this well-written post, Smith shows the truth behind the amplifying effect of technology on the networked society (Van Dijk 2012), and the 'culture of real virtuality' (Castells 1996), by which is meant the very real influence of many non-physical or digital aspects of our society. It also shows that the students are using social media to communicate with their professor and other students in both online and offline environments simultaneously. Whilst proponents of this type of behaviour are likely to see the advantages of students sharing questions and answers, and to celebrate the utilisation of technology during face-to-face interactions in order to reach a much wider audience, others might wonder if the students were to put down their devices and dedicate their full attention to their professor, would this help them more than the fragmented Q&A sessions they seem to be having? Many people would certainly argue that the fragmentary nature of these conversations is qualitatively reducing the value of face-to-face conversation. This is also criticised elsewhere regarding other forms of communication as an attention deficit (Turkle 2015a), 'snippet literacy' (Baron 2008, 204–6) and the inevitable consequences of information overload (Eppler and Mengis 2004). Surprisingly, a recent study by Microsoft received a lot of media coverage when it claimed that attention spans had dropped from twelve seconds in 2000 to eight seconds in 2015 as a result of increased digital device usage. This study was not peer-reviewed however and has many flaws, many of which are expertly pointed out by Porterfield (2016) in an online science blog, and also by Furedi (2015) in an article for *The Independent*. The central claim in the Microsoft study about attention is inherently difficult to prove, and even if data is collected, isolating one responsible factor over time is extremely challenging, if not impossible. There seem to be just as many studies showing the positive influence of digital devices as there are negative ones, but generally the negative articles are more widely picked up by popular media (Lynch 1996, see also Wu and Shen 2015 for the correlation between retweet popularity and negative sentiment of news).

Despite the claim that digital devices are reducing our attentions pans, scientific studies have shown many positive effects of ICT, specifically computer games (Granic et al. 2014). Psychologists have also noted that computer gamers have, if anything, an incredible ability to maintain their attention and focus. Such observations have also been made by Csikszentmihalyi (1997, 2013), which have in turn influenced a new trend in education towards gamification and edutainment (Lazzaro 2009). These methods are posited to be improvements on traditional rote-learning techniques because they are more active, and when people enjoy an activity (such as learning) they are more likely to sustain it for longer and maintain the activity over a longer period.

Of course, at the moment there is fierce debate over this issue, and the waning and waxing attention spans of our students are by no means new in educational debates. This has been dubbed as 'continuous partial attention', a term coined by software executive Linda Stone in the late 1990s. Whilst this is often used as a pejorative term, there are voices who claim that this is a much needed skill in today's world (Jenkins et al. 2009, 2013), and that this trend is a demonstration of cognitive dexterity (Rose 2010). Perhaps switching focus and multitasking is a form of media literacy which has evolved naturally as part of the restructuring of information in the networked society.

Attention deficits and multitasking can also be observed at academic conferences. I have attended many events where delegates seem to be writing notes on their laptops, phones or tablets. However, this is an oversimplification of what is actually happening amidst all this frantic fingerwork. Much of the time, people are not just taking notes, they are multitasking, checking facts, conducting quick searches, perhaps live-tweeting quotes. I saw once sat behind a famous professor and noted that he was coding whilst also paying attention to a talk. Observers in the popular media note that people now are too easily bored, and thus they seek distractions and require new stimulus even in real time (see for example Turkle 2012, 2015a, b; Carr 2010). The claim is that our online browsing habits have come to be reflected in our face-to-face interactions. In his extraordinarily prescient book, Castells (1996) predicted that these trends would also be reflected in the workplace, with many employees on flexitime, leading to an extremely segmented economy.

Many of the people I have observed at conferences working on their laptops are not merely making notes, they are broadcasting them to Social Networking Services (SNS) as the event happens in real time; another example of the amplifying effect of the network society. This is the culture of connectivity (van Dijck 2011, 2012, 2013), the reality of our polymediated existence (Herbig et al. 2015). These delegates no longer participate in plenary speeches, lectures and concurrent sessions as consumers, but also as 'produsers' (Bird 2011). This was demonstrated in the quote from Smith (2017) which I used to start this section.

As Tagg (2015) has examined in detail, the nature of our blended societies, in which digital communication has become so inextricably linked to and integrated with ordinary discourse, leads to questions about the nature of readership and authorship that require expanded definitions of these notions. In other words, readers of online texts are not merely passive recipients, they are empowered by digital media in ways that allow them to interact with the text, to share it, to link to it and makes links from it, to post comments and add their own opinions. Likewise, Tagg asks questions about the notion of authorship, addressing the common complaints that such practices devalue the traditional place of the author, that the way we read is now being altered due to shortened attention spans. This is also echoed in an article and book by journalist Nicholas Carr (2008, 2010), who argues that the internet is robbing us of our intelligence and ability to focus. However, Clive Thompson (2013) takes the opposite approach, and points out that Carr's book, *The Shallows*, cites only one actual neurological study, which was ambiguous in its findings. In fact, according to Thompson, neuroscientists cannot yet agree (and may never be able to fully understand) what types of changes are taking place in the wiring of our brains due to our interactions with technology. Our brains are inherently designed to constantly restructure themselves, and the plasticity of the brain is what allows new connections to be made and new patterns of behaviour to be learned. A brief review of academic studies on this area is provided by Naomi Baron (2008, 216–19).

Baroness Susan Greenfield (2015), a neuroscientist at Oxford University, has added to her many articles warning about the effects of technology on the brain by publishing a recent volume dealing at length with this issue. However, she remarks early on in her book that there is not enough research currently being done to determine the effects of 'screen culture' on the young mind. Another neuroscientist, Dean Burnett, critiques Greenfield's work, claiming that her 'understanding of Facebook and smartphones [seems to be] based exclusively on an over-heard conversation between two drunken advertising executives in a pub' (2013). Burnett attacks Greenfield's articles on this issue for being for-mulaic, predictable, scaremongering, and above all based on little or no hard evidence, but solely on the force of her established career. Clearly, this is an emotive issue. Parents worry about their children's develop-ment, and the idea that our brains could 'change' or incur damage from modern technology is understandably a risk that people do not want to take. And yet, there is little way of avoiding such ubiquitous technology, even if it weren't so useful and powerful. Basically, if we remove smart-phones from the next generation, they may risk being socially ostracised by their peers.

There is no shortage of opinions on these matters, although argu-ments tend to take a particular side (pro or con), when in truth what we are seeing is an altering of communicative practices, possibly an evolution where binary notions of author/reader are complexified. As dana boyd eloquently puts it, '[t]he commercial worlds that [teens] have access to may not be ideal, but neither is the limited mobility that they experience nor the heavily structured lives that they lead' (2014, 203). In other words, this is the reality, and we must be critical and cautious, yet we must also adapt our own behaviours even as we acculturate to our own technologically advancing society with its networks that amplify change (Van Dijk 2012).

I have had to question my own attitudes towards sociotechnical prac-tices, and this is perhaps one of the starting points for this research. I encountered such an issue in June 2014 when I attended a conference in Kyoto. After my talk, given to a small audience of about fifteen people as a concurrent session, one of the participants (Cameron) came to me and told me that he had taken a great picture of me during the pres-entation, which he proceeded to show me on his phone (Fig. 3.1). At first, I mistakenly thought he was asking permission to post the photo on Twitter, but actually he had already live-Tweeted the photo and several quotes from my session, and was showing it in order for me to see that

Fig. 3.1 Picture taken during my talk in Kyoto and live-Tweeted

he had done me the favour of increasing my reach via his own social network connections. At first, I felt that my privacy had been invaded, but I quickly realised that I had been speaking publicly to a room of delegates, and that made my image, my words and my ideas fair game for wider dissemination through SNS, as long as the proper attributions were made. I remember this incident very clearly (and the photograph helps with retention), and in particular I was struck by the need for me to reassess the notion of ownership over my image and words. Upon reflection, it is ironic that behind me is an image I was using on my slides which I also do not own copyright over, and yet I was happy to use it in my presentation.

When I was in Argentina in August and September 2017, it was my first experience to be the keynote speaker and as such my image was shared and disseminated even more widely. But, by this time I was much more well-prepared, although it was alarming to see how many images of me found their way onto social media. However, it is not only during public speeches that these issues occur. The famous case of Zhang Zetian, aka Sister Milk Tea, is a good example. A photograph of the girl drinking milk tea went viral in 2009, and now she is one of China's wealthiest and most well-known celebrities. Another example is the

Technoviking, whose dance moves lead to a viral video, and subsequently a court case over personality rights, culminating in a fascinating documentary named *The Story of Technoviking* (2016) about the issue of identity, privacy and online sharing.

Whether such acts are indeed violations of privacy has been a matter of increasing debate, and here augmented communication is playing an important role, as privacy becomes a central issue during such face-to-face interaction where online and offline selves are blurred, and where personal interactions that happen in real time are published and amplified through the web and given a digital rendering, which include the interpretations, biases and other affective filters of the uploader(s). This is further amplified by context collapse (Marwick and boyd 2011).

As I proceed through the description of each type of augmented communication, these issues will begin to be more foregrounded, especially as we approach types of augmented communication which specifically blur the boundaries between online and offline, physical space, and synchronous and asynchronous interaction.

3.1   Examples of Augmented Communication in Daily Life

In the following sections, ethnographic and autoethnographic data are presented from my ongoing research into the area of augmented communication. I will present key examples of augmented communication which have been carefully documented and present them in context for analysis.

As I discussed in the methodology section, the observations and discussions that make up the dataset of this study were recorded initially as field notes, then worked into journals and coded and analysed. These were then further added to and reflected upon in order to arrive at four main categories of augmented communication; which are multimodal augmentation, meta-augmenting, augmented cognition and augmented participation. In the following four vignettes, I provide instances where the major categories of augmented communication are presented as examples in use. These vignettes are then expanded in Chapter 4 and outlined in detail, using the same basic structure. However, I should also point out that these categories are by no means extensive or final, and there may be contexts in which they overlap.

3.1.1   Vignette One: What Type of Dog Have You Got?

An example of multi-modal augmenting. Showing personal pictures from a smartphone in-order to enhance the conversation.

The following vignette has happened numerous times to me, with increasing frequency as augmented communication becomes more common in people's lives. The most recent occurrence at the time of writing was actually in Argentina whilst I was there for a conference in September 2017. I had become friendly with one of the other participants and we were having dinner with a group of five others, when our conversation turned to dogs somehow. When I realised that Ricardo was a fellow dog-owner, we naturally asked each other 'what type of dog have you got?' and proceeded to show pictures of our mixed-breed rescue dogs to one another. Of course, it was once common for people to carry one or two photos of their families around in their wallet or purse, but now we may have thousands of images stored on our phones, which we can use as part of a conversation. Not only do these photos work as a stimulus for conversation, they also act as a stimulus for memory as well. From my observations, this is by far the most common form of augmented communication, and there are several subcategories as well, depending on the type of image or media being shown. Later, in Sect. 5.1, I will examine the impact of showing visuals on the conversation, as well as looking briefly at how this could also affect our memory and perception.

3.1.2   Vignette Two: Zombify, FaceJuggler and Ringtones

An example of meta-augmenting. During a visit to my family in England, my 15-year-old niece and my 61-year-old father both utilise their phones in order to initiate and enhance conversations in strikingly similar ways.

It is now rather common to talk about digital devices, just as we talk about TV shows or music. What particular apps we have on our phone is just as valid a line of conversation as, say, the weather. Indeed, the news often features stories about 'trending' topics online, as well as profiling new technologies, as I will discuss in further detail in Chapters 4 and 5.

In 2012, I made some of my earliest observations of augmented communication during a visit to my family in England. Three moments in particular inspired my initial investigation into augmented communication.

The first revolves around the following photograph, which was created with an app which had just been released called Facejuggler. Now there are several apps with the same function, but in 2012 this seemed like quite a new thing. I was sitting on my Nanna's sofa with my then 15-year-old niece. She and I often have a lot of banter and as the photograph shows, she was pointing at my face for some reason. My sister, Helen, took a photograph on her phone through the app, which then swapped our faces around, creating the following hilarious, albeit somewhat disturbing, image (see Fig. 3.2). This may seem like a small instance, but the conversation around the app is itself notable for being both about mobile digital technology and for having been simultaneously facilitated by the same technology. We discussed the app whilst using it. My sister also uploaded this picture to SNS, which I will discuss later as this then becomes yet another form of augmented communication (see Sect. 4.4.3).

This alone may not have been enough to spark my interest in augmented communication. However, it was not an isolated incident. During the same visit, my youngest sister, Vicky, took a photograph of me in a pub which she put into another app called Zombify. This app then made me look like a zombie. We discussed the app as we were discussing our phones, in much the same manner that people may comment

Fig. 3.2 FaceJuggler

on an item of clothing or a worn accessory. In this way, the apps on our phone are similarly an expression of our personalities (Kant 2015). In other ways, apps can act as 'social lubricants' (Pink and Hjorth 2014, 493–94) by providing people with things to talk about. These need not only be gimmicky apps where photos are altered, but even just using Twitter or Facebook to find topics for discussion, an observation made by one of my students, Tuck, during a workgroup session after they had conducted systematic self-observation (see also Sect. 4.2.1).

It should be noted that such usage is not limited to teenagers or younger adults. My father, who was in his early sixties in 2012, also engaged in these conversations and often used his own phone for conversations as well. In a pub, my father was showing me all the different ringtones he had set on his phone, and was particularly proud that the *Jaws* theme played whenever a certain scary person called him, acting as a warning. This was a kind of anecdote and the punchline was provided by the ringtone. At the time, I remember feeling embarrassed that my dad was playing ringtones on his phone in a quiet pub, and I felt that this might have been bad etiquette, which is always something that orbits around augmented communication such as this, and the 'rules' are still unclear about what is acceptable.

3.1.3   Vignette Three: Zoltán, the Tour Guide

An example of augmented cognition. When the man who was going to lead our guided tour fell ill, another took his place by reading from Wikipedia.

In 2014, I attended a conference at the University of Nottingham. At the end of the conference, I participated in a social event which involved a bus tour around Nottingham and the surrounding area, with a few stops at places of interest such as Sherwood Forest. One of the conference organisers, Peter, had been scheduled to act as a guide for the event, as he was very interested in the area and had an encyclopaedic knowledge of its history. Unfortunately, Peter suddenly had to visit the hospital due to an eye injury. Luckily, he recovered enough to return for the conference dinner, but during the tour there was nobody to provide the audio guide. Heroically, another of the organisers named Zoltán (a distinguished professor) stepped up to lead the bus tour. During the introduction, Zoltán mentioned that, although he lived in Nottingham, he really was no expert and so he was 'reading everything off Wikipedia'. Of course, this was hilarious, and the entire event was very pleasant and enjoyable, with added comedy from the fact that Zoltán was being helped by another organiser, but they did not know how to turn off the microphone. Despite this, my lasting memory was that I was impressed with the way Zoltán was able to take Peter's place as our tour guide, and to teach us interesting facts as we drove around Nottinghamshire whilst he was himself learning on the fly. It shows that humans have a natural ability to multitask, and that we can use digital devices to tap into a repertoire of knowledge and information quite seamlessly during conversation. As I have already introduced, such a resource is referred to as 'exomemory' (Baym 2015, 26), and, like literature and film, this acts as a repository for experience and knowledge which would ordinarily be beyond the reach of an un-networked individual.

3.1.4   Vignette Four: News of My Father's Triple Bypass Surgery

An example of augmented participation. When I called my father to ask the results of his angiogram, my sister was already there and I was able to join their immediate discussion despite being over 6,000 miles away. At the same time, comments were pouring onto social medial offering consolation and support. In this way, the offline/online realms are blurred.

The final vignette serves to demonstrate how the lines between online and offline are often blurred, making an essentialist distinction between the two realms a 'false dichotomy' (Tagg 2015), certainly at least in terms of identity construction.

For some time, my father has been suffering from shortness of breath, and in September 2017 he had to cancel his visit to see us in Japan because his angiogram results indicated that he would need triple bypass surgery. Whilst still in the waiting room, he was unable to take calls, but he texted me via Skype the bad news, and then more or less copied and pasted the same message for a more general audience on his Facebook feed. A few hours later, after he was out of the hospital, I was able to call him on Skype for a video chat. My sister, Vicky, was also there and we discussed the operation, offered our support privately, whilst asynchronously having posted supportive messages and 'liked' the messages of others who were also expressing their concern and lending their good wishes. During the video call, we sometimes discussed these messages in order to cheer my dad up, saying things like 'did you see that comment by so-and-so', as some of my dad's friends had written humorous posts, perhaps due to the 'ludic' nature of much online discourse (Deumert 2014).

Despite the fact that few studies have examined the emotional aspect of mobile phones, Vincent and Fortunati (2014, 312) claim that mobile devices 'are contributing and strengthening the emotional glue that keeps the fabric of society together'. This stands in stark contrast with recent claims by Sherry Turkle in her books *Reclaiming Conversation* (2015a) and *Alone Together* (2012), which present ethnographic observations alongside other published research implicating digital devices in a decrease in empathy and the ability to have meaningful interactions. However, far from being disconnected, apathetic, apolitical or disengaged, researchers such as danah boyd have shown that today's networked youths are actually very much engaged and connected. In her book *It's Complicated: The Social Lives of Networked Teens*, boyd (2014) demonstrates artfully how teenager's online and offline identities are part of a complex continuum of social interaction, and the two cannot be separated.

Quite often what we mistake for a disconnect can easily be explained by knowing the full story. In the book, boyd tells the story of Taylor, who moved to Boston and befriended Chris and Corey. When Taylor and Corey started dating, Chris became jealous and began displaying aggressive and bullying behaviour to Taylor, both online and offline, even going so far as to vandalise her school locker. When the school authorities became involved, Chris was heavily punished due to the school's zero-tolerance policy towards bullying. However, in fact Chris was gay and having a difficult time coming out. Only Taylor knew about this, and she knew Chris was interested in Corey. Taylor felt sorry for Chris, and did not see his acts as bullying because she knew more than she could tell the school, as she had to keep the secret of Chris's sexuality confidential (boyd 2014, 134–36).

Who are we to say that someone is disconnected just because they look at their phone during talk? A similar thing happens when we go to restaurants and observe an older couple who are sitting in silence. The knee-jerk reaction is to assume the couple have nothing to talk about, that their love has died but they remain together through complacency or perhaps fear. The reality may be so, but it may equally be that they are simply comfortable together enough to enjoy a moment of silence.

Indeed, such moments, where we can be 'alone together' giving one another space, are necessary in sustaining long-term relationships.

The truth about phones and their impact on conversations such as this is likely to lie somewhere in the middle. In this way, my father and sister were able to augment their conversation by bringing in a third participant, who was also able to provide moral support for a difficult situation. Furthermore, the comments coming in asynchronously online through SNS further enhance these sentiments and help to build a sense of community. I doubt that these digital participators were seen as interruptions in this context, but in others they may be seen as such. I believe we simply need to accept the importance of social context when making judgements about augmented participation and the way this influences the dynamics of ongoing face-to-face interactions.

3.2   Further Examples: Authenticity, Identity and Connectedness

Although there is research to suggest that a different aspect of one's identity might emerge through online interactions, and that discourse patterns are often altered in ways which empower less vocal members of the speech group, much of this research has been brought into question. In the early days (1980s and 1990s) of CMC research, findings showed that computer conferencing evened out the playing field of communication and allowed people a voice who ordinarily had lesser linguistic capital and were lower on the organisational hierarchy (Sproull and Kiesler 1991). However, the picture is now more complex, and several studies have shown that power relations, issues of control and other features of face-to-face discourse are still manifest in CMC. Indeed, as Baron notes, 'CMC researchers began to realize that online communication hardly guaranteed either social or gender equity' (2008, 52).

Our online identity is of course merely an extension of our offline identity, as several scholars have clearly demonstrated (see for example boyd 2014). The same rules apply as for how we construct and maintain our multiple selves through contextual and socially constructed performances (Seargeant and Tagg 2014a). The issue of authenticity is important when discussing both face-to-face and online interactions, and there are multiple nuanced meanings and interpretations of the word authenticity as it applies here. For Turkle (2012, 2015a), authenticity is an essential aspect of making conversations meaningful, personal and fulfilling. She discusses the issue of authenticity in relation to robots, and the relationships between humans and machines. In the collection by Seargeant and Tagg (2014b), authenticity is discussed by Page (2014) in relation to impersonated identity and online hoaxes. Elsewhere, I have also discussed authenticity online in relation to digital culture (Pinner 2016b, 150–55), and in terms of managing online identity (Pinner 2016a). I will revisit these issues in more depth during the discussion in Chapter 5. For now, it is important to note that in augmented communication, the line between online and offline is much more blurred than in other forms of discourse. Indeed, the false dichotomy of online vs offline is very much apparent during augmented communication, as our embodied self interacts with the digital; our media literacy is utilised as we carry out the performances which construct our identity. In Chapter 5, I will further examine how this implicates the digital divide, and the place of digital literacy in augmented communication.

Our conversations on SNS do not take place only online, and indeed SNSs and social media are extremely powerful tools with their own ecosystem (Hanna et al. 2011) and political power (Shirky 2008, 2011). Although careful to note the key role it played during the 2011 Egyptian revolution, Agger criticises Facebook and other SNSs for being inane, made up mainly of 'everyday trivia' and featuring so many posts along the lines of 'I had enchiladas for dinner' (2012, 20). In an interesting version of this, my own father began using Facebook a lot more in 2016, having had an account which he barely used since 2009. Previously, he rarely wrote status updates or uploaded things, and his timeline was populated by what was posted to it by my sisters and me, or the occasional tagged photograph uploaded by a friend. Around the time he began to use the site a lot more, he posted the following status update from 9 June 2016:

> Nice to see my daughters and granddaughter tonight, [...] Went to the Fish shop for tea - very good - a real cut above your normal fish and chip shop.
>
> Bugger, I've fallen into the Facebook trap of thinking that other people are actually interested in what I had for tea!
>
> Of course, my big news today is that my second Land Rover Lightweight restoration project moved on a leap when it started and ran for a few seconds before I noticed it was dumping all its oil on my garage floor. Still, at least I know it runs. I'm hoping to have it finished in time to take it to the Masham Steam Fair on July 17.

This post received twelve replies, and started a dialogue on 10 June between my father and two of his friends, who were together at the time also working on a Land Rover. Alastair explains that he is currently with Bruce, and in this way my father's participation with his friends' physical meeting is augmented asynchronously through SNS, what I refer to as augmented participation. It is also used to arrange and enquire about another physical meeting; when they refer to 'Masham' they are talking about Masham Steam Rally, an open-air weekend event where people bring vintage cars, steam engines and other restored vehicles to show and compete.

Although not in 2016, I was present at the Masham fair in 2017 when my dad met his friends again, Alastair and Bruce. Here I recorded another interesting instance of augmented communication, specifically augmented cognition and the use of exomemory and digital literacies combined with multi-modal augmenting. Bruce announced that he was moving house and, when the others asked where his new house was, he used Google Maps to show the exact location as well as pictures. He also showed the estate agent's online listing of the house. This was an extremely enlightening observation for me, as these men are in their 60s (Alastair is actually in his 70s), they are all very much interested in 'hands on' and mechanical things, we were in a field in rural England, and yet augmented communication occurred very naturally here in quite a specific instance involving Google Maps. It is likely that the already existing closeness between these three men is why they were comfortable using their phones during an informal conversation like this, and why Bruce felt happy to pass his own phone around so the others could see where he was moving house. Another factor was that both my dad and Alastair knew the area, and so it was meaningful to them. Although present, my sister, Helen, and I were not included in this part of the conversation and the phone was not passed to us (Fig. 3.3).

As I argued at the very beginning of this book, showing pictures increases the immediate authenticity of conversations by providing a clear visual cue which can aid both understanding and retention of contextual information. This is especially important if the visual is actually necessary to the understanding of the conversation, which I demonstrate with an example in Sect. 4.1, when a colleague showed me a picture of a Japanese television celebrity who I had never heard of, but who she claimed resembled one of our co-workers. In this way, digital devices are as important to the conversation as the topic itself, and discourse evolves naturally around the potential uses of the technology.

Fig. 3.3   My father and his friends use Google Maps to talk about a new house

3.3   Summary

Chapter 3 has presented four vignettes which illustrate the wide scale saturation of augmented communication in my own life, as demonstrated through local and contextualised events observed. I have observed different people in different contexts using their phones to alter conversations in ways which would not be possible without a digital networked device. Of course, as I mentioned in the methodology section, making broad generalisations from small-scale ethnographic data is unwise, and thus these vignettes not only provide the basis for the categories of augmented communication which follow in Chapter Four, they also highlight the need for further research into this area and especially the social, linguistic and psychological issues which surround it.

3.3.1   Reflection

Readers are invited to examine their own lives for evidence of augmented communication and to observe how it affects the conversation and the different ways it is used.

REFERENCES

Agger, Ben. 2012. *Oversharing: Presentations of Self in the Internet Age, Framing 21st Century Social Issues.* New York: Routledge.

Baron, Naomi S. 2008. *Always on: Language in an Online and Mobile World.* Oxford: Oxford University Press.

Baym, Nancy K. 2015. *Personal Connections in the Digital Age, Digital Media and Society.* Cambridge, UK: Polity Press.

Bird, S. Elizabeth. 2011. "Are We All Producers Now? Convergence and Media Audience Practices." *Cultural Studies* 25 (4–5): 502–16. https://doi.org/10.1080/09502386.2011.600532.

boyd, danah. 2014. *It's Complicated: The Social Lives of Networked Teens.* New Haven, CT: Yale University Press.

Burnett, Dean. 2013. "The Only Susan Greenfield Article You'll Ever Need." *The Guardian.* Accessed October 25. https://www.theguardian.com/science/brain-flapping/2013/apr/09/susan-greenfield-article-how-to-guide.

Carr, Nicholas. 2008. "Is Google Making Us Stupid? What the Internet Is Doing to Our Brains." *The Atlantic.*

Carr, Nicholas. 2010. *The Shallows: What the Internet Is Doing to Our Brains.* New York, NY: W. W. Norton.

Castells, Manuel. 1996. *The Rise of the Network Society,* vol. 1, *The Information Age: Economy, Society, and Culture.* Padstow: Blackwell.

Csikszentmihalyi, Mihaly. 1997. *Finding Flow: The Psychology of Engagement with Everyday Life.* New York: Basic Books.

Csikszentmihalyi, Mihaly. 2013. *Flow: The Psychology of Happiness.* New York: Random House.

Deumert, Ana. 2014. "The Performance of a Ludic Self on Social Network (ing) Sites." In *The Language of Social Media: Identity and Community on the Internet,* edited by Philip Seargeant and Caroline Tagg, 23–45. Basingstoke: Palgrave Macmillan.

Eppler, Martin J., and Jeanne Mengis. 2004. "The Concept of Information Overload: A Review of Literature from Organization Science, Accounting, Marketing, MIS, and Related Disciplines." *The Information Society* 20 (5): 325–44. https://doi.org/10.1080/01972240490507974.

Furedi, Frank. 2015. "Age of Distraction: Why the Idea Digital Devices Are Destroying Our Concentration and Memory Is a Myth." *The Independent,* October 11. http://www.independent.co.uk/life-style/gadgets-and-tech/features/age-of-distraction-why-the-idea-digital-devices-are-destroying-our-concentration-and-memory-is-a-a6689776.html.

Granic, Isabela, Adam Lobel, and Rutger CME Engels. 2014. "The Benefits of Playing Video Games." *American Psychologist* 69 (1): 66.

Greenfield, Susan. 2015. *Mind Change: How Digital Technologies Are Leaving Their Mark on Our Brains.* London: Random House.

Hanna, Richard, Andrew Rohm, and Victoria L. Crittenden. 2011. "We're All Connected: The Power of the Social Media Ecosystem." *Business Horizons* 54 (3): 265–73.

Herbig, Art, Andrew F. Herrmann, and Adam W. Tyma (eds.). 2015. *Beyond New Media: Discourse and Critique in a Polymediated Age*. London: Lexington Books.

Jenkins, Henry, Sam Ford, and Joshua Green. 2013. *Spreadable Media: Creating Value and Meaning in a Networked Culture*. New York, NY: New York University Press.

Jenkins, Henry, Ravi Purushotma, Margaret Weigel, Katie Clinton, and Alice J. Robison. 2009. *Confronting the Challenges of Participatory Culture: Media Education for the 21st Century*. Cambridge, MA: The MIT Press.

Kant, Tanya. 2015. "FCJ-180 'Spotify Has Added an Event to Your Past': (Re)Writing the Self Through Facebook's Autoposting Apps." *The Fibreculture Journal* 25 (Apps and Affect). http://dx.doi.org/10.15307/fcj.25.180.2015.

Lazzaro, Nicole. 2009. "Why We Play: Affect and the Fun of Games." In *Human-Computer Interaction: Designing for Diverse Users and Domains*, edited by Andrew Sears and Julie A. Jacko, 155–76. Boca Raton, FL: CRC Press (Taylor Francis Group).

Lynch, Aaron. 1996. *Thought Contagion: How Belief Spreads Through Society*. New York: Basic Books.

Marwick, Alice E., and danah boyd. 2011. "I Tweet Honestly, I Tweet Passionately: Twitter Users, Context Collapse, and the Imagined Audience." *New Media & Society* 13 (1): 114–33. https://doi.org/10.1177/1461444810365313.

Page, Ruth. 2014. "Hoaxes, Hacking and Humour: Analysing Impersonated Identity on Social Network Sites." In *The Language of Social Media: Identity and Community on the Internet*, edited by Philip Seargeant and Caroline Tagg, 46–64. Basingstoke: Palgrave Macmillan.

Pink, Sarah, and Larissa Hjorth. 2014. "The Digital Wayfarer: Reconceptualizing Camera Phone Practices in an Age of Locative Media." In *The Routledge Companion to Mobile Media*, edited by Gerard Goggin and Larissa Hjorth, 488–98. London: Routledge.

Pinner, Richard Stephen. 2016a. "Constructing and Managing Transportable Identities on Social Networking Sites." *Explorations in Teacher Education* 23 (2): 2–5.

Pinner, Richard Stephen. 2016b. *Reconceptualising Authenticity for English as a Global Language*, edited by David Singleton, SLA. Bristol: Multilingual Matters.

Porterfield, Andrew. 2016. "Another Modern Myth: Shrinking Attention Spans." Genetic Literacy Project. Accessed October 14. https://geneticliteracyproject.org/2016/07/25/another-modern-myth-shrinking-attention-spans/.

Rose, Ellen. 2010. "Continuous Partial Attention: Reconsidering the Role of Online Learning in the Age of Interruption." *Educational Technology* 50 (4): 41–46.

Seargeant, Philip, and Caroline Tagg. 2014a. "Introduction: The Language of Social Media." In *The Language of Social Media: Identity and Community on the Internet*, edited by Philip Seargeant and Caroline Tagg, 1–20. Basingstoke: Palgrave Macmillan.

Seargeant, Philip, and Caroline Tagg (eds.). 2014b. *The Language of Social Media: Identity and Community on the Internet*. Basingstoke: Palgrave Macmillan.

Shirky, Clay. 2008. *Here Comes Everybody: The Power of Organizing Without Organizations*. New York, NY: Penguin.

Shirky, Clay. 2011. "The Political Power of Social Media: Technology, the Public Sphere, and Political Change." *Foreign affairs* 90: 28–41.

Smith, David. 2017. "Teaching in the Age of Social Media." [Website]. University Affairs, Last Modified April 5, 2017. Accessed October 13. http://www.universityaffairs.ca/career-advice/career-advice-article/teaching-age-social-media/.

Sproull, Lee, and Sara Kiesler. 1991. *Connections: New Ways of Working in the Networked Organization*. Cambridge, MA: MIT press.

Tagg, Caroline. 2015. *Exploring Digital Communication: Language in Action*. London: Routledge.

Thompson, Clive. 2013. *Smarter Than You Think: How Technology Is Changing Our Minds for the Better*. New York, NY: Penguin.

Turkle, Sherry. 2012. *Alone Together: Why We Expect More from Technology and Less from Each Other*. Philadelphia, PA: Basic books.

Turkle, Sherry. 2015a. *Reclaiming Conversation: The Power of Talk in a Digital Age*. New York: Penguin Press.

Turkle, Sherry. 2015b. "Stop Googling. Let's Talk." *The New York Times*, SR1. http://www.nytimes.com/2015/09/27/opinion/sunday/stop-googling-lets-talk.html.

van Dijck, José. 2011. "Flickr and the Culture of Connectivity: Sharing Views, Experiences, Memories." *Memory Studies* 4 (4): 401–15. https://doi.org/10.1177/1750698010385215.

van Dijck, José. 2012. "Facebook and the Engineering of Connectivity." *Convergence* 19 (2): 141–55. https://doi.org/10.1177/1354856512457548.

van Dijck, José. 2013. *The Culture of Connectivity: A Critical History of Social Media*. New York: Oxford University Press.

Van Dijk, Jan. 2012. *The Network Society*, 3rd ed. London: Sage.

Vincent, Jane, and Leopoldina Fortunati. 2014. "The Emotional Identity of the Mobile Phone." In *The Routledge Companion to Mobile Media*, edited by Gerard Goggin and Larissa Hjorth, 312–19. London: Routledge.

Wu, Bo, and Haiying Shen. 2015. "Analyzing and Predicting News Popularity on Twitter." *International Journal of Information Management* 35 (6): 702–11.

CHAPTER 4

Types of Augmented Communication

Abstract This chapter provides an overview of the ways smartphones (and other devices) are utilised to enhance face-to-face communication in real time during personal exchanges. It offers a look at the way context and relationship also affect the dynamics of augmented communication. Each type of augmented communication is illustrated with at least one contextualised example from autoethnographic data. Where possible, an indicator of the relative frequency of each type is provided, although these are merely indications.

Keywords Digital communication · Face-to-face interactions · Technology · Language · Applied linguistics · Sociolinguistics

Following on from the previous chapter, which presented four vignettes alongside other examples situating augmented communication in use, this chapter explains more broadly each of the four categories. As explained in the methodology section, these categories were arrived at inductively, through a process of multilayered analysis of autoethnographic observations. The four categories that emerged were; (1) multimodal augmentation, in which various types of media are displayed to the interlocutor; (2) meta-augmenting, in which people discuss the technology whilst demonstrating; (3) augmented cognition, in which speakers utilise *exomemory* from the web and other networked repositories to further conversations in different ways, and finally;

© The Author(s) 2019
R. S. Pinner, *Augmented Communication*,
https://doi.org/10.1007/978-3-030-02080-4_4

49

(4) augmented participation, in which users add other speakers via either video or text, to enter into conversations from other geolocations both synchronously and asynchronously.

4.1   MULTIMODAL AUGMENTATION

This section details augmented communication in which multimodal media (such as images and videos) are shown during conversations in order to enhance or augment the discussion.

Multimodal in the sense used in this book comes from the concept of multimodality; the use of various modes to produce a single message. Modes can be visual, textual, linguistic, anything which can convey a semiotic message. Multimodal media can generally refer to digital media which utilise several semiotic modes within a single artefact. In other words, the conversation becomes multimodal when mobile digital devices are employed to add pictures, video, audio and other types of media as an additional stimulus to augment the discussion being had.

In my dataset, multimodal is the most common form of augmented communication, and I have frequently observed such forms of conversation in societies where smartphones are common. This is likely to be a consequence of our polymediated society, a natural aspect of convergence culture and the way that transmedia has become part of our everyday experience (Herbig et al. 2015). This may be because our identities are highly bound up with the participatory media with which many people interact daily, spending hours of their time reading and interacting, and in some cases relying on knowledge of online trends to remain up-to-date in certain types of speech community.

Because multimodal augmentation is now so pervasive in my data, it is necessary to further delineate it according to the type of media being shown or used, and the way the conversation envelops them. From my observations, I have identified three distinct types of multimodal augmentation, although there may be others which arise or need to be further distinguished as our understanding of augmented communication deepens. These three types are firstly, showing pictures, which can also be divided further between images and personal photos; secondly playing videos and thirdly playing audio or music.

What follows is a detailed description of each variation, accompanied by observations and illustrative examples.

4.1.1   Visuals

In the following sections, I will look at the use of visuals as part of augmented communication, differentiating between *personal photos* (user-generated) and more generic *images* which come from a broader range of sources.

4.1.1.1 Showing Pictures

> A father is someone who carries pictures in his wallet where his money used to be—anonymous

The above quote is clearly an old joke dating from presumably the twentieth century. However, the quote, despite its having been widely shared and even becoming an internet meme, has begun to seem somewhat dated in the last four or five years.

The possession of a smartphone means that it may no longer be necessary for people to carry photos with them, as they can easily have thousands stored on their devices. It is a long time since I heard any comments about the old stigma attached to inviting someone to come and view a slideshow of your holiday photos, although as a child growing up in the 1980s I remember such jokes being common. When people I know have been on holiday, what they tend to do is take out their phone, swipe quickly through the gallery until they find the set of images needed to illustrate their spoken topic, and then begin flipping through. Sometimes only one image is shown, but often they might even show an array of pictures in a kind of pop-up, ad hoc slideshow. I frequently observed this type of augmented communication in my data, and for many of the people I spoke to, it does not seem strange to use their phones as part of a face-to-face conversation if they are showing pictures to others. I would speculate that this is now quite a natural reflex for communities with high smartphone permeation. In my observations, I have noted that people will either flash through their photos, pausing usually for less than a second on each picture, or they will actually hand the phone or digital device to their interlocutor, who can then swipe through the pictures at their own pace. The latter action seems more likely to occur between close friends as there is obviously a chance that other images might be reached, and handling another person's phone is a sensitive matter of privacy and etiquette. Some of the respondents in my data had different views about the matter of touching another person's phone, indicating an area for further research.

As recently as the year 2000, the trope of the 'boring slideshow' was still very much alive and well in western culture. An episode of the US sitcom *Friends* demonstrates this, when Ross shows Rachel's sister a slideshow of his favourite fossils in *The One Where Chandler Can't Cry*. With augmented communication, the showing of multiple pictures can potentially be much more interactive than the slideshows of before, and people can even zoom in using the now ubiquitous pinch feature on most touchscreens.

The most recent example I have observed at the time of writing was just yesterday, when I showed two friends I have not seen in over a year some slides from my recent visit to Argentina. I showed personal photos of Iguazu Falls and other scenes from a conference I had attended. Notably, these two friends were at the time, not connected with me on Facebook and so they had not seen the photos beforehand. Showing the pictures as I described my trip provided an added visual stimulus, an immediate authenticity through the picture which places the interlocutor in visual space as we tell our stories or provide verbal descriptions. Writing for *Forbes* magazine, McCoy (2017) explains that visuals are altering the way marketing is approached, with consumers apparently voicing a preference for visuals over written text. Furthermore, in studies with English as a foreign language (EFL), Lin and Chen (2007) found that using visuals greatly improved learners reading comprehension ability, mainly due to the fact that the visuals were thought to facilitate the activation of schemata (pre-existing knowledge links in the mind). The visuals reduced the cognitive effort of retrieving the stored schemata, and thus more attention could be paid to the reading task. There is very convincing evidence that visuals aid learning, memory and comprehension, as well as having the added weight of impact (Graber 1990; Fekete et al. 2008). Language accompanied by visuals is more persuasive, more memorable, more immediate and more powerful than mono-media delivery. Studies have shown that stories accompanied by pictures have the power to influence opinions, and carry 'emotional consequences' (Powell et al. 2015, 997). Multimodal communication like this was very commonplace in ordinary face-to-face conversations through augmented communication, as many of my participants seemed to feel this was quite an everyday occurance for them.

Of course, there are very real implications of this type of communication, as the use of visuals alters the way we perceive and remember conversations. This will be discussed in more detail in Chapter 5, especially Sect. 5.1, where I will discuss how visuals can influence memory and have an increased effect on interlocutors.

Personal Photos

Unlike images, personal photos are user-created and usually have been taken with the phone's camera. They are used for both personal and professional reasons during conversation.

The most common and easily observable type of augmented communication from my data is showing pictures, and often these are personal photos, or other user-generated pictures. I label these more general types of digital pictures as Images, so as to be more general and encompassing. In this section I present several examples of people talking to me and using their phones to show personal pictures.

In Fig. 4.1, Griselda from the Ministry of Education shows me a photograph of her son and a mutual friend. I had only just met Griselda a few days before at a conference, and she had then invited me to Buenos Aires to give a workshop. In the restaurant afterwards, we were talking over lunch and when the phones came out I began explaining my research.

In Fig. 4.2, my wife and her friend show one another the professional photos of our families taken for the *shichi-go-san* coming of age celebration. The two interlocutors are both in their early 30s, and quite close friends through having children the same age. This picture was taken while we were observing my son's swimming lesson in late September 2017. What is interesting here is the characteristic solidarity building of

Fig. 4.1 Augmenting in Buenos Aires

Fig. 4.2 Augmenting in Tokyo

female discourse (Romaine 2000). My wife's friend told her about the photos, and so my wife also showed our photos, demonstrating a sense of unity and affiliation, something which is often attributed as being characteristic of female speech (Tannen 1991).

Additional data comes from my workgroup lessons. In one particularly interesting comment, a student from my linguistics seminar shared the following observations:

> When I was working part-time at a public bathhouse last Tuesday, an elderly woman asked me by what age little boys could get in women's bath. After I answered the question, she started talking about her grandson who had just turned 3 years old and showed me some pictures of his birthday party. This is what I told during last class. Today she came back again, so I asked her how her grandson was doing. This time she showed me a new video of him to let me see how energetic and cute he was. (Student X, 10/10/2017)

This example is particularly interesting, as it shows that an elderly stranger who is merely a customer at a bathhouse can feel comfortable showing pictures on her phone. In doing so, this customer builds a relationship with the staff member (my student). It becomes a talking point, and the multimodal augmentation no doubt helps this customer stand out from others and remain more familiar, thus developing a sense of belonging within this small and developing community. This is important as there are interesting differences in phone etiquette for gender and age (Forgays et al. 2014). When Student X told me about the first of these two incidents, it was during a seminar just after the first systematic self-observation task. I asked Student X if this customer were a regular patron of the bathhouse, to which she replied no. By the time Student X posted her observations on the discussion forum, the second incident had happened, suggesting that the lady may now be planning to become a regular customer. This can also be inferred by her initial question, about what age she can bring her grandson. It seems clear that she felt validated and comfortable enough to show pictures of her family on her phone. I feel that this is important, as clearly the situation, context and nature of interlocutors seem to be vital factors in multimodal augmented conversations.

Some of the students from my workgroup lessons told me that they are sometimes hesitant to use their phones, even just to show pictures, when they do not know a person well or when they are in more formal situations. However, it seems that when multimodal augmentation is utilised, it can foster tight bonds or strengthen existing connectivities between people. Essentially, in showing an array of private images, we are letting people into our private worlds, and we are often enacting different transportable identities (Zimmerman 1998) of ourselves in other contexts to show other sides of identity.

This happens in both personal and business settings too. For example, on the 18th of July 2017 I was on a flight to Amsterdam from Manchester when I found myself observing four men at the airport, one of whom was showing photos and videos on his phone. I noticed them as we queued to board the plane, and it turned out that I was sat behind three of them, with the fourth man being sat by the window next to me. These men appeared to be on a business trip. From their accents, they were all English, with ages ranging from perhaps early twenties to early forties for the more senior man, who was presumably the boss. Like me, they were probably changing at Schiphol airport, and from their conversation it seemed to me they were heading somewhere in the Middle East, where they were going to be working with heavy industrial machinery. In particular, these men were talking about drilling large holes in the ground. Ordinarily, such a conversation would not interest me, but I found myself eavesdropping as all of the men, but particularly the most senior, were using their phones as part of the conversations they were having. Also, as occasionally the fourth man sitting next to me would be involved, it was not easy to ignore their conversation as they would even pass phones between the aisles of the seats.

The boss was showing pictures on his phone and even short videos which were related to their work. In particular, he was showing pictures of large deep holes, and commenting on the sheer scale of the industrial machinery that people were using at their destination. At one point, another man began talking about a colleague, and one of the men did not seem to remember this man. After looking at a photo of the colleague, the other man realised that he did know this mutual acquaintance, but not well. The two younger men started having their own conversation, and after a long time of showing many pictures of big holes, finally the boss realised he needed to send an email and began to work on his phone. The conversations all finally and naturally died away shortly after, with each man either reading or looking at their phones. I made careful notes of this occasion, as it seemed to me at the time that this was a good example of how power relations are still present in augmented communication, and most likely the other men would not have shown pictures on their phones unless the more senior man had done so first, although this is just conjecture for now based on personal observations.

In much the same way that we construct our ideal identities with our online profiles and posts, we of course do much the same thing in face-to-face interactions too, by presenting aspects of our identity and constructing ourselves as multifaceted people by enacting various transportable identities (Zimmerman 1998). As with many phenomena in the networked society, such practices are amplified by our polymediated age (Herbig et al. 2015) and due to issues such as context collapse (Marwick and boyd 2011). For example, a friend who I see in person only occasionally may actually see my posts on SNS daily, and so it can sometimes be a surprise that people know more about us than we had expected based solely on face-to-face interaction (Seargeant and Tagg 2014; Pinner 2016). Although perhaps to a lesser extent, we also invoke multiple aspects of our identities when we present images and pictures that we find interesting, as I will explain in the next section.

Images and Other Visuals
In this book I use the term Images to describe non-user generated visual content, usually selected from online sources, such memes or trending

topics for example. I frequently observed people sharing such images on their phone, especially if this is part of the conversation and the other party has not seen the image in question, for example sharing memes. I also recorded that, after showing an image on one's phone, people might be asked to forward the link to the image, so that the other person can find it and share it also.

At times, showing an image is part of the process of authenticating a conversation, or including someone who otherwise would not be able to join in. An example of this happened to me in late September 2017, when out with a few colleagues. One of my colleagues was telling me about a famous actor who looks like another of our colleagues (who was across the table in another conversation). I was joining this conversation half-way through, and so I needed to be caught up. The others in the group were laughing already as they knew the actor, and in their heads they could see the comparison. However, I did not know the actor, so my colleague found images of him through a google search, and sure enough there was a kind of resemblance (see Fig. 4.3).

What interests me in this instance was that my colleague wanted to include me in the conversation, and without the prior knowledge of this actor, I would not be able to get the joke or authenticate their discussion. Sensing that this was essential to continue the conversation, my colleague naturally turned to her phone to augment the conversation. At the time, I had not mentioned anything of my research into this area to her, so this data arose very naturally in that respect. In this way, my colleague was also accessing exomemory through Google image search, in order to find examples that she needed to enhance my understanding and provide me with the necessary information to join the conversations.

4.1.1.2 Playing Videos

Less common than showing pictures but still highly widespread in my dataset is the sharing of videos and communal watching of them during face-to-face interactions.

Showing videos occurs in much the same way as showing pictures and images, especially with user-generated content as both photos and videos tend to be stored and accessed through the same gallery app. In February 2017, YouTube announced on its official blog that users spend over one billion hours per day watching videos online through the site. The announcement triumphantly continues:

Fig. 4.3   Lookalike

Let's put that in perspective. If you were to sit and watch a billion hours of YouTube, it would take you over 100,000 years. 100,000 years ago, our ancestors were crafting stone tools and migrating out of Africa while mammoths and mastodons roamed the Earth. (YouTube 2017)

When I was in a rural village in North Yorkshire, England, near my hometown on 22 March 2017, I visited a local pub in order to (ostensibly) prepare for my upcoming Ph.D. viva. I found myself making copious notes of augmented communication, and one of the events was a group of five men in their mid to late thirties or early forties. Although the pub was quiet and it was just after lunch, they were watching a comedy video together on their phones. Although the volume was loud, I couldn't make out what the video was, but the men were laughing together and saying 'oh, he'll love that'. From snippets of the conversation, it seemed they were planning a stag night and were going to show this video on a large screen during the event. One of the men said 'send us the link'. At the time, my notes recorded that these men were oblivious to the fact that this could easily be seen as rude behaviour, as the excess noise disturbed the atmosphere of the pub. However, for them, this was a social activity, and they discussed the online videos as a form of multimodal augmentation, without considering the other patrons of the pub.

Of course, we can further distinguish videos by recognising some are user-generated content and others may be videos that we either stream or download to our devices. Again, it is important to note that there will be personal videos and ones used for professional purposes as well, just as we distinguished between images and pictures, which is why I include both pictures and videos under the broader category of visuals. A point worth noting is the way people share non-user generated content such as videos and static images. This may be a natural extension of television watching. Previously, people had to tune in at the same time and to the same channel to catch a programme or show. Now, we have a myriad of watching options, many of them geared around the user making selections in their own time, such as Netflix and YouTube. Other more user-generated videos also reach a wide audience as they go viral and are shared across a wide array of SNS, which I have also observed can become talking points, just as people talk about television shows. Watching the video on a mobile device during the conversation can attain the immediacy of authenticity, making the conversation more focused. Again, the consequences of this will be discussed in more detail in Chapter 5.

4.1.2   Playing Audio/Music

My participants often share music or play other audio during conversations. Listening to audio seems to be less common than watching videos in my data, but it does happen and is therefore worth mentioning.

In my observations, it is not always easy to tell if I am seeing augmented communication with audio, or if what I am actually witnessing is merely people listening to music out loud on their phones whilst talking about something else or engaged in another activity. For instance, in a café in the rural English town near where I was born in North Yorkshire, I was annoyed by two young teenage girls who were playing music through their phones whilst doing their homework. Both girls were listening to chart music, and they code-switched between two languages, so it was not possible for me to fully catch how much of their talk was about the music. What I do remember was feeling irritated as there was already music playing from the café, and their music was loud and tinny. It is indeed common for people, at least in the UK, to play music through their phones without speakers even though they are in public places. This would not count as augmented communication, of course, but it is relevant as it involves the etiquette of mobile devices. Such practices contribute to the widespread belief that phones are making people worse at communicating. I will discuss the issue of etiquette in Sect. 5.4.

Of course, there are times when audio and video are merged, such as in a music video. Again, the premise of incorporating multimodal digital media is very much the same and I merely mention it here for consistency. In general, this section is presented as delineating between certain types of media and certain modes, but the main point is that my participants use them all in much the same way, showing visuals as a way to enhance the immediate authenticity of a conversation and augment spoken discourse with other semantic modes. Now that I have listed the major types of multimodal augmentation, I will move onto other types of augmented communication. The next type involves taking a step back from the conversation in order to make phones part of the conversation in terms of both topic and augmenting.

4.2   Meta-Augmenting: Using ICT and CMC to Talk About ICT and CMC

This section details augmented communication in which users discuss digital devices, exchanges which took place online, or other examples where the topic focuses on Information Communication Technology (ICT) or Computer-Mediated Communication (CMC).

As I have already discussed, when we use multimodal augmentation, we draw on the resources of exomemory in order to further our face-to-face conversations. However, due to the central role of technology in our modern lifestyles, my participants also discuss technologies even as we use them.

Meta-augmenting is another product of our highly digital society. Just as people talk about TV shows, music, the news and other current affairs, people now also talk *about* their phones whilst simultaneously using their phones to augment the conversation. The vignette I provided in Sect. 3.1.2 was a clear example of this. Having a new app on our phone is not only useful for whatever service the app performs, it is also a conversation piece. Of course, not everyone I talk to cares to hear all about the apps I use regularly, and so this type of augmented communication tends to take place between more digitally literate or technologically inclined people, or those for whom the phone is a more central aspect or an extension of their personalities rather than a mere accessory. I have some friends who are simply disgusted at the mere mention of a trendy new app, whilst others can happily discuss their phones without feeling that we are being 'nerds'. I noticed that the people I talk apps with most are my sisters and my niece, who I see in person rarely enough anyway as I live in Japan and they live in England, and so most of our interactions are mediated through SNS (generally Facebook) and apps (increasingly more WhatsApp) in the first place, which is quite possibly the reason for this. This would be an area for further study, and certainly warrants further investigation.

4.2.1   *Sites and Hypertext*

Users discuss a particular site or piece of hypertext as part of conversation, often reading and speaking at the same time.

In my observations, people discussed websites, blog posts and other forms of hypertext in much the same way that they might talk about a newspaper or magazine article. The difference is that, whereas we are unlikely to retain newspapers or magazines and carry them with us for conversational purposes, hypertext is easily accessible and usually remains available indefinitely through networked media. I observed people showing these sites so as to aid their memory or check facts as they reiterate them.

Several of my workgroup lesson students reported that they use their smartphones as note-taking devices. I have also observed some people (mainly university students in Japan) using the image roll of photos they have taken on their phone as their 'to do' list. When someone tells them of an interesting page, they either take a photo, or open a tab in their browser and then keep that tab open to look at again later. I first observed this in Kyushu in 2015 when I visited Kyushu University to see a friend and give a short talk. During dinner afterwards I got into a conversation with a young woman who worked for the university. She was asking me to recommend films for her to watch, and as I spoke she opened new tabs for each film. She also gave me several recommendations, and I used my phone to take notes in the same way. Thus, I seemed to have mimicked the augmented communicative behaviour, which then became part of how I use augmented communication myself.

Another way that hypertext is used during face-to-face conversation was brought to my attention by the observations of a student in my linguistics seminar from the workgroup lessons. Tuck made the following remarks about his use of hypertext:

> When someone's conversation is boring I tend to pull out my phone and go on Twitter or Facebook. I realized this is an act of search for a new interest for the ongoing uninteresting conversation. This action makes the conversation to be more interesting because I bring the content out from the online source. (Tuck, 13/10/2017)

Turkle (2015) also describes having observed this phenomenon. It could seem alarming that people use their phones to escape boring conversations. Perhaps, in some cases, looking at a phone is a passive-aggressive act, or meant as a sign that the conversation is uninteresting. Turkle is highly critical of this strategy of discourse as she sees it to be a sign of not just shorter attention spans, but more perniciously, a disconnect from authentic and heartfelt communication (Turkle 2015). She describes how young people scroll through their phone, looking for new topics to talk about, how they constantly seek entertainment and are terrified of boredom. This need to be constantly stimulated, as she sees it, also impacts on people's ability for solitude and self-reflection, she argues. For her, the simultaneous use of digital devices during conversations, even just to show pictures and images, indicates the shortening of human attention through technology and the facilitation and exacerbation of an empathy gap. These matters will be discussed at more depth in Chapter 5.

Information online can also be used to expand a person's knowledge and utilise exomemory to perform other types of augmented communication, which I discuss in Sects. 4.3. An example of this was given in the introduction, when I mentioned Chiyori-san, the retired Geisha.

Drawing on resources available to us through digital devices, conversations can move into areas where we learn things even as we discuss them by accessing stored information (exomemory) or by utilising literacies that enable us to learn on the fly.

4.2.2   Apps

Users discuss the actual apps on their phones and demonstrate their functionality as part of the conversation. Apps may also be used as part of the conversations without being directly related to the subject—for instance, using the IMDB (internet movie database) app to discuss films.

Goldsmith (2014) provides a detailed overview of the mobile app economy and the various ecosystems within it. He explains that in 2013, first Apple and then Google both announced having passed the 50 billion app downloads milestones on their respective stores. This demonstrates that apps are actually a veritable industry with a multibillion-dollar revenue. On Japanese TV Asahi, a panel-show hosted by Takeshi Kitano named *shiranai nyūsu* (news you didn't know [from around the world]) features a regular section which showcases amazing apps, as well as viral videos and other topics from the world's media which are trending. Not only are there scores of dedicated YouTube channels for reviewing apps, but there are also countless blogs which recommend various apps, editors' picks and other dissemination and filtering services that have sprung up in order to help people navigate the immense number of options on offer for apps. My research indicates that, another way that people share and learn more about apps is through face-to-face conversation.

During Vignette Two, I demonstrated specifically how apps on our phone might become talking points during face-to-face conversations. The importance of apps is gradually becoming more obvious, as they constitute not just an important part of the new socioeconomic and sociotechnical 'like' economy, but they are also purportedly able to 'facilitate and enhance new modes of user self-expression' (Kant 2015, 31). In other ways, apps can act as 'social lubricants', as they do for research participant Michelle in Pink and Hjorth's (2014) study, which looks at users' cameraphone practices in social settings. This study highlights the importance of mobile digital devices as communicative props. In the study, Michelle notes that 'nothing perks up a difficult social encounter more than fatify! [an app that makes you look fat]' (2014, 493–94). The paper mentions several encounters which could all be classed as different forms of augmented communication, including using the act of taking selfies and uploading them to SNS as a way to have conversations during a train ride with a new acquaintance. Meta-augmenting is also described several times in Turkle's book, *Reclaiming Conversation* (2015). For example, she describes her meeting a group of twenty-five young people (aged between 18 and 24) who are in Boston for summer study.

> During our two hours together they tell me that if I really want to know how they communicate, I should be in their group chat. They are having it on an application for their mobile phones called WhatsApp. They invite me into their group, I accept, and our meeting continues. Now we are together in the room and online. Everything changes. […] In the room, the topic turns to how hard it is to separate from family and high school friends during college. But it is hard for this discussion to go very far because it is competing with the parallel activity of online chat and image curation.
>
> Yet I see how happy these students are. They like moving in and out of talk, text, and images; they like the continual feed. (Turkle 2015, 35–36)

After making this observation, Turkle becomes critical of this pattern of discourse, claiming that the conversation never goes anywhere because the participants are 'always elsewhere'. She argues that these participants are terrified of boredom, and their constant search for stimulation robs them of an awareness of the present moment and the ability to connect meaningfully with each other in it, which she terms the 'Goldilocks effect'. Whilst many of Turkle's observations are poignant, this one in particular I found problematic based on the evidence she cites. First of all, she fails to account for her own role as an ethnographer, her own contribution to the social dynamic. She has just met these people, there are twenty-five of them in the room, and of course in two hours' people can't realistically be expected to open up as much, especially in a formal research setting with an outsider sitting in on them. Turkle's criticism of the conversation is that the twenty-five young people fail to draw on their own experience, which strangles the interaction of a deeper personal connection and starves it of significance, but I feel that sharing images in the way she describes *is* a form of sharing personal experience. If we take the theory of extended mind into consideration (see Sect. 4.3), these young people's identity and experience is made up just as much from external experiences as it is from internal ones. We do not live and experience life in a vacuum but are constantly influenced by things outside of 'us' which we internalise and draw into ourselves. I also discuss this in Sect. 4.2.4, when I talk about digital culture, sharing memes and animated GIFs.

4.2.3 Social Media and Augmented Gossip

Users show SNS feeds, comments and uploads as part of the conversation. Often, this becomes a form of 'gossip' in the sense that the discussion involves people known to the interlocutors without directly involving those people about whom they are speaking.

As the previous section attempted to show, apps are often talking points for people, and the immense range in functions they provide means that they can facilitate a huge variety of conversations. In much the same way, social media is in and of itself a talking point and item worthy of discussion. Not only is this reflected in our conversational practices face-to-face, but also in the news and current affairs too. What we call 'news' is no longer the sole domain of journalists and newspapers or radio and television; it is now greatly shaped by online sites and blogs, by individual users with large followings (Jenkins et al. 2013). There are even websites, such as klout.com, which quantify users' online reach. This reach can be monetised by 'liking' and 'sharing' selected products on their SNS profiles, with users with higher ratings receiving higher rewards (van Dijck 2013, 76). In 2012, Facebook founder and CEO, Mark Zuckerberg, announced in a status update that monthly users had exceeded one billion. Now this figure has risen to 1.23 billion daily (statista 2017), and Twitter sees around 500 million tweets per day (internet live stats 2017).

> Twitter's ambition to be an echo chamber of serendipitous chatter thus finds itself at odds with the implicit capacity, inscribed in its engine, to allow some users to exert extraordinary influence. (van Dijck 2013, 74)

Such is the power of SNS that it is now possible to see examples of what could be called 'meta news', where established newspapers report on what is currently trending online; in effect making news out of the news. The BBC website has a section entitled 'trending', which covers items currently being discussed. *Forbes* magazine also has a social media section, which provides updates and analysis about what is being covered in social media. In fact, a great many major news providers feature regular stories reporting on trending topics under discussion in social media.

Aside from trending topics being a talking point which will often lead to augmented communication as people use their digital devices to provide immediate authenticity for topics under discussion, social media is also a part of embodied conversations as friendships evolve in face-to-face interactions. I noticed several examples of this during my observations. When I visited Singapore in May 2016, I met and became friends with several new people who lived in different parts of the world. One of the first things we did during a social gathering for dinner and drinks was to add each other as 'friends' on Facebook. I noted at the time that I felt this was actually a good way of ensuring that everyone knew each other's names. During the conference we had all been wearing lanyards with our names and affiliations on them. When we left the campus where the conference was being held, we naturally took them off. Adding people on social media meant that we had a good reason for confirming that everyone knew who everybody else was. It did not feel awkward or like an invasion of privacy to be in a situation where we all added one another. Furthermore, once added, we noticed that some of us had mutual friends, which we would not have known otherwise. The world became a lot smaller through this simple act, and our group bonded very closely during those few days and we have all remained in fairly regular contact, although I have not seen any of those people again in person since.

Similarly, the year before, when I had visited Hong Kong, I was recognised by someone who I was connected to through the academically oriented SNS academia.edu. Also, when I registered for the conference and collected my lanyard and conference programme, I was again recognised as one of the few people who had 'liked' many of the pre-conference posts which had been put on the conference's Facebook page. In this way, our online interactions are expanding our face-to-face ones asynchronously, making social interactions possibly smoother through the creation of familiarity and shared conversational topics. In a way, this provides a schema of potential talking points for face-to-face interactions. Although it has been noted that new technologies have the potential to make people more socially anxious through decreased eye-contact and actual in-person interaction (Reece and Danforth 2017; Lup et al. 2015), it may also be that establishing a schema in the way just described could actually alleviate the precursors for social anxiety. This seems like a fruitful area for further research.

Finally, the act of utilising social media during face-to-face interactions leads to another type of discussion; a form of gossip which is augmented through networked connections. In a recent social evening in September 2017 where I met two friends who I rarely see, we noted that we were not 'friends' on Facebook yet, even though the three of us had known each other and kept in touch for several years. We proceeded to add each other there and then (see Fig. 4.4). What followed was an interesting discussion, in which we 'gossiped' about various people we knew, facilitated by our newly networked friendship. Although I define gossip here as mere idle talk about others known to us but not physically present, I should also like to note that this was not destructive or defamatory talk. Indeed, gossiping is now thought to be a fundamentally sociopsychological endeavour which is deeply seated in our nature as humans. Dunbar (1996) has famously suggested that gossiping was essentially part of the evolution of language, arguing that it creates and strengthens social bonds.

Of course, there is a downside to social media and its applications to face-to-face interactions. The first is that, when we check our phones, we open up the risk of distractions from the present moment. There are etiquette issues as well, not just in phone usage but also in the way we may ask someone for friendship on social media. There have been times when I felt almost as if I was under duress when someone wanted to find my profile on social media. It can create potentially face-threatening situations. Finally, there is also the potential for cyberbullying, cyberstalking and cyber harassment, all of which augment face-to-face situations which

Fig. 4.4 Friends become 'friends'

are unpleasant. In this way, our social media identities and interactions need to be carefully managed, just as our offline identities are

4.2.4   Memes, GIFs, News and Digital Culture

Users discuss popular or current topics as they emerge, news items or recent trends. This is especially the case if the speakers are both users of a particular forum, regular visitors to a particular site, or utilise SNS to read news and gain access to other forms of information.

As briefly touched upon earlier, an additional aspect to meta-augmenting is that this trend is also visible in a wider sense in the news and popular media. Meta-news, as I have called it, is a product of our information-saturated societies. The news itself is now more participatory in nature, not just in terms of commenting and discussion, but also in terms of actually reporting and recording events (Deuze et al. 2007). People often record events on their phones, which then become the footage used in news reports. The immediacy of the phone camera and relatively good quality of these portable image capturing devices means that emerging stories can still be covered without necessarily sending a reporting team out to the scene of an event. The immediate authenticity of news events is actually *captured* by mobile digital devices. Twitter in particular, has begun to feature heavily not just in the news and mainstream journalism, but also in the academic literature on journalism as well—see for example Ahmad (2010), Hermida (2010), Broersma and Graham (2012, 2013) for further discussion.

In the previous section on apps (4.2.2), I quoted Turkle's observations with a group of young people in Boston, in which the group augmented their conversation through WhatsApp. Turkle notes that:

> At least half of the phone chat takes the form of images – cartoons, photos, and videos – many of which comment on the conversation in the room. As the students see it, images connect them, equal to any text or any talk. (Turkle 2015, 35)

Although this is mere conjecture, it seems reasonable to imagine that a large portion of the visuals being shared in this manner would be internet memes and GIFs. The word *meme* was first coined by Richard Dawkins, in his book *The Selfish Gene*. He refers to them as 'self-replicating' ideas' (1976, 255) and 'self-replicating patterns of information' (1976, 431).

This concept was developed in 'esoteric forums and message boards, where participants first linked Richard Dawkins' (1976, 1982) theories of cultural replication to shared in-jokes, catchphrases, and signature texts' (Milner 2016, 1). Internet memes are now an easily recognisable and widespread phenomenon, typically (but not always) incorporating a central image with a caption of text both above and below the image. A difference between memes and genes is that memes are based on mental processes and acts of observation. As Davison points out, '[t]he meme is subject to interpretation and therefore to variation' (2012, 122).

Memes in digital culture are an additional aspect of the online world of trending topics. Just as we discuss current affairs and trends, we also discuss and share memes in face-to-face conversations. In some ways, when the meme is humorous in nature (as they often are) this is merely an extension of the telling of a joke. Of course, humour is an important aspect of social bonding, and although it is often culturally specific (Medhurst 2007), the global nature of digital culture has led to its own specific brand of humour.

> Rather than simply accepting or rejecting global models, local actors combine the foreign and the familiar to create multifaceted, hybrid cultures. (Shifman 2014, 154)

In this way, the evolution and spread of memes can be mapped to Mark Deuze's discussion about the emergence of digital culture, and the intervention necessary to make sense of this mediated world, comprising of interrelated components; participation, remediation and bricolage.

1. Users become active agents in the process of meaning-making (we become participants).
2. We adopt but at the same time modify, manipulate, and thus reform consensual ways of understanding reality (we engage in remediation).
3. We reflexively assemble our own particular versions of such reality (we are bricoleurs).
(Deuze 2006, 66 [adapted slightly for clarity])

These interactions thus reshape the media world. Deuze argues that this praxis is achieved through users' agency in the cycle, which defines digital culture.

Shifman (2014) attributes memes to *user-generated globalisation*. Milner (2016) calls memes a *lingua franca* for online culture, part of the language of participatory media. Memes also show the development of online forms of written speech (Davison 2012). Replying to a prompt in one of the workgroup sessions, one participant said:

> I'm not sure if this counts as augmented communication but sometimes me and my friends reply to memes with memes. It becomes a sort of conversation with pictures. (Ivo, 22/07/2018)

Unfortunately, this is the entirety of Ivo's written message, but I do know that he decided to write his term paper about memes and also he was a mixed race youth with European heritage, similar to Tuck. I am not sure if Ivo is talking about online interactions or face-to-face, but it seems likely that he is referring to both.

At this point, I should add that I rarely show memes during augmented communication, and my other ethnographic observations reveal very few such interactions, with one possible exception being at the conference in Kyoto which I mentioned in the introduction to Chapter 3. Coincidentally, Cameron, the same person who took my photo and uploaded it to Twitter, also gave his academic presentation entirely though internet memes, which I found both effective and entertaining. From my observations, the sharing of memes is mainly an online activity which happens through SNS, although this is only my own experience. During one of the workgroup lessons, one of my students commented on the fact that internet memes were not particularly big in Japanese culture, and she did not really know what memes were until she went to the United States for study abroad. My own observations of the use of memes in face-to-face conversations are mainly limited to discussions with young white males living in Japan, Japanese youths with experience living abroad (such as Tuck whose comments I presented earlier), or during visits back to the UK.

It seems fitting that Milner (2016) equates memes with the cultural vernacular of the networked society. There is a discoursal quality to memes; they evolve in response to one another, spurring reproduction and interpretation much like spoken interactions. In a recent large group discussion I engaged with on Facebook in October 2017, GIFs were very much used as full sentences (i.e. a discussion could be had using only memes, as in Ivo's earlier example). I was posting to a closed group dedicated to sarcasm, and I noticed that, despite Turkle's assertions that sharing images in this way means that young people no longer draw on their own experiences (2015, 35–36), I found posting GIFs gave me an opportunity to post what I felt were quite personal pieces of discourse despite not being my original work. By sharing GIFs from, for example, the classic British sitcom *Blackadder*, I revealed identifying hints about my age group and nationality, and an aspect of my own personal taste in humour. I felt that posting a *Blackadder* GIF was more refined than those of some of the other users, and that doing so gave me the opportunity to perform parts of my identity whilst at the same time revealing very little of actual value to a group of asynchronous strangers. Perhaps in this way, memes and GIFs allow people to invoke transportable identities that draw on cultural products which act almost as *exo-identity*, in much the same way we draw on exomemory through networked devices. Whitney Phillips also notes in her discussion of online trolls that despite their anonymity, people 'wore their nationalities like a World Cup soccer uniform' (2015, 77). In this way, perhaps we can share and discuss memes and other images, and this slowly feeds our networks (both face-to-face and online) publicly dispensable and non-face-threatening pieces of our identity which we are willing to disclose as we develop a deeper bond.

4.3   Augmented Cognition

Humans have always relied on external resources in order to go beyond the physical limits of their bodies, and to extend the processing power and storage capacity of their minds. Take Isaac Newton's famous quote from a letter to Robert Hooke in 1676, in which he said 'if I have seen further it is by standing on the shoulders of Giants'.

In today's networked societies, users conduct searches in order to learn about something relevant to the immediate conversation in real time. As this takes place, one interlocutor generally assumes the role of teacher/learner whilst the other participants listen and provide further questions or express their understanding through other discourse features. Such practices have already led to search engines like Google being referred to as a form of *exomemory* (Baym 2015, 26). I expand on this theme, differentiating between exomemory and digital literacies. Combining these two resources, I argue that types of augmented communication which utilise digital devices for exomemory and digital literacies could be called augmented cognition.

The term augmented cognition already exists, and was originally referred to as the act of 'increasing the capability of a man to approach a complex problem situation, to gain comprehension to suit his particular needs, and to derive solutions to problems' (Engelbart 1962). However, it has now become associated with more integrated technology featuring direct interface between cognition and computers.

> Augmented cognition is a form of human-systems interaction in which a tight coupling between user and computer is achieved via physiological and neurophysiological sensing of a user's cognitive state. This interactive paradigm seeks to revolutionize the manner in which humans engage with computers by leveraging this knowledge of cognitive state to precisely adapt user-system interaction in real time. (Stanney et al. 2009)

At present, most of the research into augmented cognition seems to be at the military level, and it mainly concerns itself with identifying differences in cognitive states due to the pressures of in-the-field decision-making, and the subsequent 'successful transition of these cognitive state gauges to operational military human-machine systems' (St. John et al. 2004). Often, the term is abbreviated to AugCog, especially for military usages. Naturally, there is much controversy over the issue, not just because of its military applications, but also due to the difficulties in applying such neurophysiological technologies to living humans. However, in my observations, augmented cognition has been taken up as a natural product of having tools in our pockets which are at our disposal during conversations where we draw on exomemory in order to maintain a conversation, check something or win/lose an argument.

Although I run the risk of associating augmented communication with military-level neurophysiological research, I use the term augmented cognition much more loosely, to refer to the fact that people are now much more likely to utilise exomemory during conversations by googling things on their smartphones. I realise that this may seem quite far removed from the research into AugCog which is currently underway, and yet I find the term fitting if we adopt a more general definition, in much the same way that augmented communication is an adapted form of AAC. As discussed in Chapter 1, Andy Clark, has already made a convincing case that we are *natural-born cyborgs*, positing that the human mind 'simply cannot be seen as bound and restricted by the biological skinbag' (2003, 4). Acknowledging the common association that a cyborg features silicone chips and computers within a biological humanoid body, he extends the definition convincingly to apply to modern humans.

> My cat Lolo is not a natural-born cyborg. This is so, despite the fact that Lolo (unlike myself) actually does incorporate a small silicon chip. [....] The presence of this implanted device makes no difference to the shape of Lolo's mental life or the range of projects and endeavours he undertakes. [...] By contrast it is our special character, as human beings, to be forever driven to create, co-opt, annex, and exploit nonbiological props and scaffoldings. We have been designed, by Mother Nature, to exploit deep neural plasticity in order to become one with our best and most reliable tools. (Clark 2003, 6–7)

Clark is developing this concept from his (and others') work on embodied cognition and the extended mind; an idea that rejects the dualistic[1] view of mind and considers how the body influences the mind just as the mind influences the body. In this way, cognition is situated, it is part of our being-in-the-world which is informed by our coping and dealing with present reality (Anderson 2003). In this way, augmented communication and augmented cognition seem appropriate terms for the way we exploit external tools to further our conversations in face-to-face interactions. As Clark also notes, 'the human brain is a past master at devolving responsibility' (2003, 25), referring to the way we utilise tools and ever-new technologies to reduce the cognitive load on our brains, potentially freeing up mental processing resources for higher-order thinking.

In the popular Netflix animation *Rick and Morty*, I have noted several instances of augmented cognition. The very first pilot episode, for example, sees Morty recite the square root of Pi. His father, Jerry, who would not be expected to know such information, quickly takes out his phone and googles it, only to express surprise that his son was right. In another example, from episode nine of season one (entitled *Something Ricked This Way Comes*) Morty and his father, Jerry, are working together on a science project which is a model of the solar system. Jerry suggests using a ping-pong ball to represent Pluto. Morty tells his father that Pluto is not a planet, which Jerry disagrees with, having learned it in the 3rd grade. Morty takes out his phone and says 'I just googled it. Pluto's not a planet', at which point he shows his father and continues 'they changed it in 2006'. These examples, having made it into popular media, hint at the permeated nature of augmented cognition in modern societies where digital devices are commonplace.

In the following sections, I will discuss in more detail the issue of exomemory and the way people rely on technologies to aid or fill in gaps in their cognition during face-to-face conversations.

4.3.1   Exomemory

Exomemory is a term that originated from the science fiction novel *The Quantum Thief* (2010) by Hannu Rahaniemi. Baym (2015) discusses the story's prescience, explaining that much of the technology envisaged in the story is already in existence or being researched. She explains that 'Facebook and Google already function as proto-exomemory' (2015, 26), but I would argue that we can already leave behind the proto-prefix, based on the previously stated argument that these technologies do not need to be integrated *under the skin* in order to be a part of us, our thinking and our way of being.

It is important to note here that the term exomemory refers to a repository of information which is stored outside our minds, usually on networks or possibly as data on digital devices. Under this definition, personal photos on our smartphone could be considered as exomemory. Other examples include sites like Wikipedia or Facebook, where information is stored for later access. This concept is not unlike that of *prosthetic memory*, which postulates that film, literature and other technologies of mass culture can expand the experiences of an individual, acting as a cultural repository of memory from which we can derive new and otherwise unavailable experiences (Landsberg 2004). However, whereas prosthetic memory is conceptualised as being part of cultural heritage and identity, exomemory is more homogenous, and refers specifically to the existence of digitally accessible media and text which can serve a purpose during speech. In her early work, Turkle acknowledged the irony in computers facilitating what she called '"informalist" ways of knowing' (1995, 52), because computers were, for a long time, seen to embody abstract thinking as opposed to being mere extensions of our memories. Later in her study, she quotes her research participant, Will, who refers to the internet as 'a giant brain' which is developing on its own (Turkle 1995, 265).

The human mind (and so-called intelligence) is not solely comprised of things locked in the grey matter of our brains, and cognition might rely on external factors just as much as internal ones. This is why we are *natural born cyborgs*, as Clark (2001, 2003) refers to us, because our extended minds have always relied, wherever possible, on forms of exomemory (memories stored outside the brain) and strategies for accessing information on the fly from external sources. In many ways, books and libraries are an example of this. Furthermore, the act of writing itself is a way of externalising our thought processes. The very act of writing a note or making a list quite often means that I do not need to refer back to it. The process of having logged a note creates a mnemonic connection in the mind because of the additional cognitive processes that have been undertaken through the act of writing. In this way, exomemory is just a new label for a very old human strategy for extending our cognitive abilities beyond the physical limitations of our brains.

I have made countless observations of interlocutors conducting ad hoc searches on their phones. The most common feature is to simply google something during a conversation in order to learn more about it. During my workgroup lessons, students often told me that they rely on their phones to choose a place to eat, find the best way to get somewhere (using GPS and online maps) and even during lessons, students are checking facts and sometimes they are even instructed to do so by their teachers. I am not the only person to do this in my institution, and I have even spoken to students at another Japanese university who told me that their 65-year-old Japanese literature teacher often asks his students to google things during class in order to learn more about the topic. When people search for facts or look things up by themselves, this increases their cognitive involvement and is less passive than merely being told the information, which is hypothesised to lead to longer and deeper retention (Laufer and Hulstijn 2001; Hulstijn and Laufer 2001). This issue is also discussed during the analysis section in more detail in Chapter 5, with particular focus on Working Memory and the concept of exomemory.

Turkle has also observed ad hoc searches which utilise exomemory, and she writes of them disparagingly. In her research, she encountered a fifteen-year-old girl whose father wanted to check the name of a film director during a meal with her. The girl, Chelsea, said 'Daddy, stop Googling. I want to talk to you' (Turkle 2015, 104). For Turkle, this is a defining point in her argument about how phones are destroying quality family moments. She also recounts various incidents in which young children beg their parents for attention, pleading with them not to look at their phones. Such accounts are certainly heart-wrenching. In Japan, there is a children's picture book (based on an essay by a Singaporean high-school student which went viral), called *mama no sumaho ni nari-tai* [I want to be mama's smartphone]. In the book, published in 2016 by Nobumi, a boy is constantly competing for his mother's attention, and he believes she pays more attention to her phone than to him. At school, his teacher asks people what they want to be when they grow up. The main character, Kantaro, says he wants to be a smartphone, so that his mother will notice him. In my workgroup data, one student who I shall name George posted the following in our discussion forum

> Last weekend, I went to a pub with my dad, and while drinking I noticed a number of cocktails that I didn't know. I naturally asked my dad if he knew any. He responded that he did, but he just told me to look it up on my iPhone. He felt- to be honest so did I- it was easier and faster to just look it up on the Internet. Apparently it was now old school to go through the hassle of explaining things when you could get the accurate information online in seconds. With pictures too! (George, 25/07/2018)

Of course, if children are feeling neglected by their parents due to excessive phone usage, or if googling a fact during a conversation to learn the answer is seen as disruptive to the conversation, this is extremely bad. However, there are times when utilising exomemory in this way actually enables the conversation to move further, and to move into new areas which could not be reached without access to networked information. The example of Chiyori-san which I discussed at the start of the book in Sect. 1.4.1 is one such occasion, as is the one provided in Vignette Three. A further way that conversations are enhanced through digital devices is by actually adding people into the conversation through augmented participation, thus expanding the audience and enabling face-to-face conversations to transcend time and space.

4.4   Augmented Participation

As we sense our inner diversity we come to know our limitations. We understand that we do not and cannot know things completely, not the outside world and not ourselves. Today's heightened consciousness of incompleteness may predispose us to join with others. (Turkle 1995, 261)

The final category of augmented communication is augmented participation, a term which is already in use and generally refers to participating in live events through online media. During augmented communication, participation in the conversation can also be augmented either in real time or asynchronously, using either text, voice or video link. In this way, the geophysical and temporal boundaries of conversations are expanded, and people are able to participate in face-to-face interactions (even attend conferences, debates and concerts) with the aid of technology. This was previously demonstrated in the quote by Smith (2017) which I presented at the start of Chapter 3. This is perhaps one of the oldest forms of augmented communication, and although my data suggests that adding people via video link is rather uncommon to ordinary face-to-face interactions, participation through text via social media is quite a frequent and natural event in many conversations, often taking place alongside meta-augmenting as a by-product of these types of conversation.

4.4.1 Joining by Proxy: Bringing Someone into the Conversation via CMC

When we meet friends and engage in face-to-face interactions, if a mutual friend is nearby, on the way, or not present for some other reason, it is quite acceptable to check digital devices to see where they are. Facebook introduced a 'check-in' function to the site in 2010, which allows people to use geotagging to add a status update with their present location. This can then become a talking point, especially if other friends are tagged, which naturally leads to others commenting, posting messages or photos, and possibly even deciding to join in person if the situation allows it.

The image in Fig. 4.5 shows my recent Facebook check-ins from Puerto Iguazu in Argentina. It shows who I was with, and then mutual friends of both parties are able to 'like' and comment. Sometimes this brings in third parties known to all of those featured in the primary check-in site, but at other times (and very often) people known to only one of the primary party may see and comment as well. This is an example of context collapse, and indicates the complexity of online/offline networked relationships.

This happens both synchronously and asynchronously, across geolocations and even transcending various levels of social interconnectedness, meaning that augmented communication which utilises this form

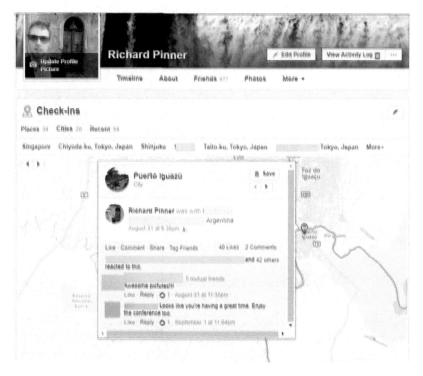

Fig. 4.5 Augmented participation

of extended participation can spread events and discussion through time and space to a much wider audience than previously possible before the networked society. It is also possible to add people to conversations in real time, as I will discuss in the next section.

4.4.2   Adding Faces in Real Time

This section examines how friends and colleagues in other geolocations are added to the conversation via VOIP, commonly utilising video-conference technology and speakerphone.

Although it occurs infrequently in my data, at times a small number of my participants indicated that they may add an additional person to a face-to-face conversation through phones using video conferencing tools, such as Skype or Facebook Messenger. In my own personal observations too, this is something I encounter quite rarely. One of the students in my workgroup lessons commented that she had experienced this. She explained:

> My friend and I were talking about another friend, and my friend used her phone to call the other friend so we can have a conversation with three of us. (Rione 10/10/2017)

According to Rione, this friend often calls or adds others to conversations like this, but she herself has never added a face in real time. This is, of course, rather distinct from a video-conference call or a pre-arranged video-chat. A more frequently occurring pattern in my data was to add a person into an ongoing conversation using text, in order to allow for participation asynchronously and at each participants' convenience, as I examine in the next section.

4.4.3 Adding Synchronous/Asynchronous Members Through SNS

As discussed above, augmented communication can also be used to expand a physical meeting into online territory, often by 'checking in' which allows others in the network to add comments either synchronously or asynchronously. This is especially common when members of a network meet up, especially having crossed geolocations.

Aside from being a talking point in its own right, social media and SNS also provide an interesting medium where online and offline discourse can begin to blur. A conversation that starts on Facebook may be continued when people meet face-to-face, or vice versa, as happened with the Facejuggler example. I previously linked this to the creation of schemata for conversations (Sect. 4.1).

After my sister, Helen, had taken the photograph discussed in Vignette Two, she uploaded it to Facebook, tagging both me and my niece. When I came back to Japan, I noticed that there were comments on this picture, and in this way we continued the discussion online through SNS asynchronously. In this way, the conversation was able to extend itself beyond the immediate time and space, and furthermore others who were not present at the original moment were also able to contribute. The same also happened with my father and his friends who were working on a Land Rover (Sect. 3.2). In some instances, such conversations may continue asynchronously, spanning months or even years—especially with new features in many SNSs which retrieve old posts from several years ago, such as Facebook's *On This Day* feature.

4.5   Summary

This chapter has presented the four main categories of augmented communication in greater detail, alongside situated and contextual examples and breaking each main type down into further sub-categories. All of these were based on my observations and a systematic analysis of them over time. Several issues surface as I discussed these categories, which were discussed in relation to some of the relevant literature.

I feel it is important to remember that phones and other mobile networked devices themselves are not inherently designed to devalue face-to-face conversation, just as they are not designed to augment face-to-face interactions either. It is reductive and essentialist to claim that these technologies are creating an effect upon the users, and it shifts the onus away from society in general and onto the spectre of 'technology', a term even more general and ethereal than the so-called 'digital native'. These patterns of use have evolved due to human ingenuity, finding new and novel uses for existing tools. Some of the practices that come under the umbrella of augmented communication could be seen as disruptive to the conversation in some contexts, and as productive in others. Therefore, a critical approach, embedded in context and based on specific examples which cannot be generalised or blanket-applied to society is needed. In the next chapter, I will reflect further on the issues raised in this chapter, and attempt to step back in order to provide a level-headed discussion of both the pros and cons of augmented communication.

There is always a possibility that those writing accounts which essentialise the issue of digital devices' effects (either adverse or positive in a binary manner) are being influenced by confirmation bias; the process by which we subconsciously tend to seek out information which supports that which we already believe, which I discuss further in Sect. 5.3.

Turkle is an experienced researcher, and at one time a great proponent of the digital or *Second Self* (1995, 2005). She displays an astute awareness of both the good and the bad side of technology, for example in her TED talk from February 2012, *Connected, but alone?* she begins with an observation acknowledging how a good-luck text from her daughter made her feel so happy, and the possibility of technology to connect us with those far away. Her main fear revolves around how technology's long reach makes us neglect those in front of us. However, boyd explains that:

> When teens turn to networked publics, they do so to hang out with friends and be recognized by peers. They share in order to see and be seen. They want to look respectable and interesting, whilst simultaneously warding off unwanted attention. They choose to share in order to be part of the public, but how much they share is shaped by how public they want to be. They are, in effect, *digital flâneurs*. (boyd 2014, 203)

In other words, it is easy to forget or to fail to appreciate just how integral the issue of context collapse is to us in this networked society, where connections are amplified and extended though online social media. The term *digital native* to describe those of us born into such a world (originally attributable to Rushkoff (1996) and Barlow (1996), rather than Prensky (2001)), is actually rather reductive as a concept and even 'dangerous' (boyd 2014, 197) as it does not adequately capture the complexities and multifaceted nature of identity and the way it intersects with sociotechnical dynamics of interaction. It lends itself to the kind of generalisations that we find in mass media, making us think of an entire generation as being homogenous. Turkle also avoids using this term, as she has a profound understanding of the way the digital self interacts with the multifaceted reality of human identity.

4.5.1   Reflection

Here, I would like to invite the reader to reflect on their own instances of augmented communication. How would you categorise these various types of interaction as they occur in your experience? How pervasive is the phenomenon? To what extent do context, identity and community, as well as social relations play a role in the way you use digital devices during face-to-face interactions?

NOTE

1. Anderson explains that dualism is often inaccurately attributed to Descartes, but that it is in fact part of a long line of inquiry dating back to Plato.

REFERENCES

Ahmad, Ali Nobil. 2010. "Is Twitter a Useful Tool for Journalists?" *Journal of Media Practice* 11 (2): 145–55. https://doi.org/10.1386/jmpr.11.2.145_1.

Anderson, Michael L. 2003. "Embodied Cognition: A Field Guide." *Artificial Intelligence* 149 (1): 91–130. https://doi.org/10.1016/S0004-3702(03)00054-7.

Barlow, John Perry. 1996. "A Declaration of the Independence of Cyberspace." Electronic Frontier Foundation. Accessed October 28. https://www.eff.org/cyberspace-independence.

Baym, Nancy K. 2015. *Personal Connections in the Digital Age, Digital Media and Socitey.* Cambridge, UK: Polity Press.

boyd, danah. 2014. *It's Complicated: The Social Lives of Networked Teens.* New Haven, CT: Yale University Press.

Broersma, Marcel, and Todd Graham. 2012. "Social Media as Beat." *Journalism Practice* 6 (3): 403–19. https://doi.org/10.1080/17512786.2012.663626.

Broersma, Marcel, and Todd Graham. 2013. "Twitter as a News Source." *Journalism Practice* 7 (4): 446–64. https://doi.org/10.1080/17512786.2013.802481.

Clark, Andy. 2001. "Natural-Born Cyborgs?" In *Cognitive Technology: Instruments of Mind*, edited by Meurig Beynon, Chrystopher L. Nehaniv, and Kerstin Dautenhahn, 17–24. London: Springer.

Clark, Andy. 2003. *Natural-Born Cyborgs: Minds, Technologies, and the Future of Human Intelligence.* New York: Oxford University Press.

Davison, Patrick. 2012. "The Language of Internet Memes." In *The Social Media Reader*, edited by Michael Mandiberg, 120–34. New York, NY: New York University Press.

Dawkins, Richard. 1976. *The Selfish Gene*, 40th Anniversary ed. Oxford: Oxford University Press. Original edition, 1976. Reprint, 2016.

Dawkins, Richard. 1982. *The Extended Phenotype: The Gene as the Unit of Selection*, 1982 Edition. Oxford: Freeman.

Deuze, Mark. 2006. "Participation, Remediation, Bricolage: Considering Principal Components of a Digital Culture." *The Information Society* 22 (2): 63–75. https://doi.org/10.1080/01972240600567170.

Deuze, Mark, Axel Bruns, and Christoph Neuberger. 2007. "Preparing for an Age of Participatory News." *Journalism Practice* 1 (3): 322–38. https://doi.org/10.1080/17512780701504864.

Dunbar, Robin. 1996. *Grooming, Gossip, and the Evolution of Language.* Cambridge, MA: Harvard University Press.

Engelbart, Douglas C. 1962. *Augmenting Human Intellect: A Conceptual Framework.* Menlo Park, CA: Stanford Research Institute.

Fekete, Jean-Daniel, Jarke J. van Wijk, John T. Stasko, and Chris North. 2008. "The Value of Information Visualization." In *Information Visualization: Human-Centered Issues and Perspectives*, edited by Andreas Kerren, John T. Stasko, Jean-Daniel Fekete, and Chris North, 1–18. Berlin, Heidelberg: Springer.

Forgays, Deborah Kirby, Ira Hyman, and Jessie Schreiber. 2014. "Texting Everywhere for Everything: Gender and Age Differences in Cell Phone Etiquette and Use." *Computers in Human Behavior* 31: 314–21. https://doi.org/10.1016/j.chb.2013.10.053.

Goldsmith, Ben. 2014. "The Smartphone App Economy and App Ecosystems." In *The Routledge Companion to Mobile Media*, edited by Gerard Goggin and Larissa Hjorth, 171–80. London: Routledge.

Graber, Doris A. 1990. "Seeing Is Remembering: How Visuals Contribute to Learning from Television News." *Journal of Communication* 40 (3):134–56.

Herbig, Art, Andrew F. Herrmann, and Adam W. Tyma (eds.). 2015. *Beyond New Media: Discourse and Critique in a Polymediated Age*. London: Lexington Books.

Hermida, Alfred. 2010. "Twittering the News." *Journalism Practice* 4 (3): 297–308. https://doi.org/10.1080/17512781003640703.

Hulstijn, Jan H., and Batia Laufer. 2001. "Some Empirical Evidence for the Involvement Load Hypothesis in Vocabulary Acquisition." *Language Learning* 51 (3): 539–58. https://doi.org/10.1111/0023-8333.00164.

internet live stats. 2017. "Twitter Usage Statistics." *Internet Live Stats*. Accessed February 21, 2017. http://www.internetlivestats.com/twitter-statistics/.

Jenkins, Henry, Sam Ford, and Joshua Green. 2013. *Spreadable Media: Creating Value and Meaning in a Networked Culture*. New York, NY: New York University Press.

Kant, Tanya. 2015. "FCJ-180 'Spotify Has Added an Event to Your Past': (Re)Writing the Self Through Facebook's Autoposting Apps." *The Fibreculture Journal* 25 (Apps and Affect). http://dx.doi.org/10.15307/fcj.25.180.2015.

Landsberg, Alison. 2004. *Prosthetic Memory: The Transformation of American Remembrance in the Age of Mass Culture*. Chichester, NY: Columbia University Press.

Laufer, Batia, and Jan Hulstijn. 2001. "Incidental Vocabulary Acquisition in a Second Language: The Construct of Task-Induced Involvement." *Applied Linguistics* 22 (1):1–26.

Lin, Huifen, and Tsuiping Chen. 2007. "Reading Authentic EFL Text Using Visualization and Advance Organizers in a Multimedia Learning Environment." *Language Learning & Technology* 11 (3): 83–106.

Lup, Katerina, Leora Trub, and Lisa Rosenthal. 2015. "Instagram# Instasad?: Exploring Associations Among Instagram Use, Depressive Symptoms,

Negative Social Comparison, and Strangers Followed." *Cyberpsychology, Behavior, and Social Networking* 18 (5): 247–52.

Marwick, Alice E., and danah boyd. 2011. "I Tweet Honestly, I Tweet Passionately: Twitter Users, Context Collapse, and the Imagined Audience." *New Media & Society* 13 (1): 114–33. https://doi.org/10.1177/1461444810365313.

McCoy, Erin. 2017. "Visual Communication Is Transforming Marketing—Are You Up To Speed?" *Forbes Magazine* Online. Accessed October 18. https://www.forbes.com/sites/forbescommunicationscouncil/2017/05/12/visual-communication-is-transforming-marketing-are-you-up-to-speed/#2b-3129336f7c.

Medhurst, Andy. 2007. *A National Joke: Popular Comedy and English Cultural Identities.* London: Routledge.

Milner, Ryan M. 2016. *The World Made Meme: Public Conversations and Participatory Media.* Cambridge, MA: MIT Press.

Phillips, Whitney. 2015. *This Is Why We Can't Have Nice Things: Mapping the Relationship Between Online Trolling and Mainstream Culture.* Cambridge, MA: MIT Press.

Pink, Sarah, and Larissa Hjorth. 2014. "The Digital Wayfarer: Reconceptualizing Camera Phone Practices in an Age of Locative Media." In *The Routledge Companion to Mobile Media*, edited by Gerard Goggin and Larissa Hjorth, 488–98. London: Routledge.

Pinner, Richard Stephen. 2016. "Constructing and Managing Transportable Identities on Social Networking Sites." *Explorations in Teacher Education* 23 (2): 2–5.

Powell, Thomas E., Hajo G. Boomgaarden, Knut De Swert, and Claes H. de Vreese. 2015. "A Clearer Picture: The Contribution of Visuals and Text to Framing Effects." *Journal of Communication* 65 (6): 997–1017. https://doi.org/10.1111/jcom.12184.

Prensky, Marc. 2001. "Digital Natives, Digital Immigrants Part 1." *On the Horizon* 9 (5): 1–6.

Reece, Andrew G., and Christopher M. Danforth. 2017. "Instagram Photos Reveal Predictive Markers of Depression." *EPJ Data Science* 6 (1): 15.

Romaine, Suzanne. 2000. *Language in Society: An Introduction to Sociolinguistics*, 2nd ed. Oxford: Oxford University Press.

Rushkoff, Douglas. 1996. *Playing the Future: What We Can Learn from Digital Kids.* New York, NY: Penguin.

Seargeant, Philip, and Caroline Tagg, eds. 2014. *The Language of Social Media: Identity and Community on the Internet.* Basingstoke: Palgrave Macmillan.

Shifman, Limor. 2014. *Memes in Digital Culture.* Cambridge, MA: MIT Press.

Smith, David. 2017. "Teaching in the Age of Social Media." [Website]. University Affairs, Last Modified April 5, 2017. Accessed October 13. http://www.universityaffairs.ca/career-advice/career-advice-article/teaching-age-social-media/.

St. John, Mark, David A. Kobus, Jeffrey G. Morrison, and Dylan Schmorrow. 2004. "Overview of the DARPA Augmented Cognition Technical Integration Experiment." *International Journal of Human–Computer Interaction* 17 (2): 131–49. https://doi.org/10.1207/s15327590ijhc1702_2.

Stanney, Kay M., Dylan D. Schmorrow, Matthew Johnston, Sven Fuchs, David Jones, Kelly S. Hale, Ali Ahmad, and Peter Young. 2009. "Augmented Cognition: An Overview." *Reviews of Human Factors and Ergonomics* 5 (1): 195–224. https://doi.org/10.1518/155723409x448062.

statista. 2017. "Number of Daily Active Facebook Users Worldwide as of 4th Quarter 2016 (in millions)." *Statista*. Accessed February 21, 2017. https://www.statista.com/statistics/346167/facebook-global-dau/.

Tannen, Deborah. 1991. *You Just Don't Understand: Women and Men in Conversation*. London: Virago.

Turkle, Sherry. 1995. *Life On the Screen*. New York: Simon and Schuster.

Turkle, Sherry. 2005. *The Second Self: Computers and the Human Spirit*, 20th Anniversary ed. Cambridge, MA: MIT Press.

Turkle, Sherry. 2015. *Reclaiming Conversation: The Power of Talk in a Digital Age*. New York: Penguin Press.

van Dijck, José. 2013. *The Culture of Connectivity: A Critical History of Social Media*. New York: Oxford University Press.

YouTube. 2017. "You Know What's Cool? A Billion Hours." Official Blog, Last Modified February 27. Accessed October 18. https://youtube.googleblog.com/2017/02/you-know-whats-cool-billion-hours.html.

Zimmerman, Don H. 1998. "Identity, Context and Interaction." In *Identities in Talk*, edited by C. Antaki and S. Widdicombe, 87–106. London: Sage.

CHAPTER 5

Stepping Back: Analysis and Discussion of ICT and Language Change

Abstract This chapter takes a more holistic view of some of the issues that have surfaced throughout this book. In particular, it discusses the impact of visuals on conversation, particularly looking at how they affect the brain and memory. It then discusses the issue of exomemory in relation to working memory, and then discusses the need for critical thinking skills during augmented communication, due to the way mass media is often structured and disseminated. It discusses whether smartphones are really making us 'dumb', and finally addresses the wider existential concerns about how smartphones prevent people from being 'in the moment' or 'being there'.

Keywords Digital communication · Face-to-face interactions · Technology · Language · Applied linguistics · Sociolinguistics

As I discussed at the very start of this book, the number of new word coinages in the English lexicon has increased dramatically since 1900. In a study which used a huge corpus of over 361 billion words in English, Michel et al. (2011) demonstrated that the number of words in general usage in 1900 was around 544,000, which had increased to 597,000 by 1950. This number then almost doubled in the next 50 years, having reached 1,022,000 by the year 2000. The authors note that:

© The Author(s) 2019
R. S. Pinner, *Augmented Communication*,
https://doi.org/10.1007/978-3-030-02080-4_5

The lexicon is enjoying a period of enormous growth: The addition of ~8500 words/year has increased the size of the language by over 70% during the past 50 years. (Michel et al. 2011)

Of course, they attribute this phenomenal expansion to the undeniable impact of technology on language. As the Oxford English Dictionary stated on their blog, 'Technology remains a catalyst for emerging words' (OxfordDictionaries.com 2013). Slang and text-speech are other oft-cited examples, which have given rise to the need for the online Urban Dictionary (Smith 2011), which focuses on digital culture and modern usages. This shows a shift in the power relations of who gets to have an official say in the semantic meanings of language, of how we *codify* our reality. Naturally, a shift in the way we use language often indicates a possible shift in power, and this has very serious implications, particularly with regard to the various types of digital divide that are manifest in society. The empowering effect of technology in terms of the relationship between producers and consumers has already been discussed previously in this book (see also Bird 2011; Jenkins et al. 2013). The burgeoning fields of internet linguistics, digital humanities and other forms of online cultural study are likely to be at the forefront of this evolutionary process.

If middle-class, digitally literate people in developed countries are now using augmented communication as part of every-day face-to-face interactions, what are the wider sociolinguistic implications of this process?

One of the most lasting lessons I have taken from my autoethnographic observations is that context and individual relationships are very important when considering how augmented communication is used. Discourse is already highly dependent on a myriad of factors relating to interlocutors. Language is not only how we shape our thoughts, voice our feelings and communicate as social beings, it is also how we construct and negotiate our identity as people.

> [L]anguage is a medium of self-expression and a means of communicating, constructing and negotiating who we are and how we relate to the world around us – that is, of giving ourselves voice and identity. (Ushioda 2011, 203–4)

The importance and centrality of language in building social ties and creating a sense of our authentic selves cannot be overstated. That discourse is so highly contextualised, individual and dependent on so many social factors is well established, thus it should come as no surprise that these same rules apply when examining augmented communication.

My initial observations have revealed that people tend to augment their communication more during informal settings, or when seeking for a personal connection, although the majority of my field observations do come from personal interaction. Age does not seem to be a barrier to augmented communication, although obviously digital literacy and degree of online presence are significant factors (not to mention the digital divide and other issues such as social class and so on, both areas for deeper study in this area). Furthermore, the people in my data set use augmented communication with both friends and family members, and also with colleagues.

In the following sections, I will examine what the act of 'augmenting' means, what it might do to our brains, to our capacity for critical thinking and how digital media simultaneously works as a means of empowering those with a monopoly over information whilst at the same time providing the best weapon against such monopolies.

5.1   Impact of Visuals on Conversation

In this section, I will argue that the act of showing pictures or videos to accompany our face-to-face interactions has a powerful enhancing effect, and could potentially make a greater impact on the interlocutor than speech which does not utilise such visuals, which in turn may lead to longer-term retention. However, this impact may also make the speech more persuasive, which could be used for manipulative purposes—effectively cross-pollenating marketing strategies with personal interactions.

As users of PowerPoint and other presentation software already know, having visuals can add a great deal of impact to talks and speeches, potentially having an influence on whether people agree with the speaker's argument and find it convincing. Several studies have shown how teachers' use of PowerPoint to provide further visual stimulus and illustrate certain points can enhance lessons, with students giving higher ratings to courses and instructors that use presentation software (see for example Apperson et al. 2006). Although there are several studies which found 'no measurable influence on course performance and minimal effect on grades' (Hill et al. 2012, 243), there is some evidence that

PowerPoint is especially useful in foreign language learning classes (Lari 2014), again due to the visual scaffolding, activating schemata, and the provision of multimodal input to guide understanding.

Visual stimulus is well recognised as an important memory aid, both for initial retention and later recollection. Pictures not only aid memory, but also comprehension (Glenberg and Langston 1992). Richard Mayer at the University of California has published several papers that confirm the importance of visuals on learning, with a particular emphasis on the utilisation of technology and multimedia (see for example Mayer 2002; Mayer and Sims 1994). Importantly, there is empirical evidence that the use of pictures as a memory aid actually improves conversation and retention in Alzheimer's patients (Bourgeois 1990), with similar results being found with dementia patients as well (Bourgeois 1993). This has relevance as this form of augmented communication might also apply to non-disabled speech as well, implying that when we utilise mobile phones to augment face-to-face communication, we may be adding an additional layer to the conversation that aids later recall. I will expand on this idea more when I discuss memes and *thought contagion* (Lynch 1996).

Indeed, the power of visuals is such that there have been cases where false memories can be created in individuals by showing them doctored photographs. For example, in a study by Wade et al. (2002), people were shown a photograph of themselves flying in a hot air balloon, even though the participants had never flown in one. Half the participants constructed a false memory around the photograph and began to tell the story of how they had ridden the hot air balloon, even though the event had never occurred. The power of visuals is often utilised in learning, either by textbook publishers or teachers themselves who attempt to use a range of stimulus for their lessons, in order to engage different types of learner. This is related to the idea of multimodal input, which is now popular within education as a way of deepening learning.

5.1.1   Multimodal Input

When people are exposed to more than one type of input at a time, for instance listening to audio whilst reading the same words as text, this is called multimodal input. For example, people can 'hear faces', and in the now famous study by McGurk and MacDonald (1976), it was established that our audio perception changes based on visual cues. Studies have shown that, if we see a video of a person saying the voiced fricative /v/ sound, and yet our audio input is the plosive /b/ sound, we will 'hear' or perceive the /v/ sound. This is true even if we *know* already that we are hearing the /b/ sound. In other words, we hear what we see rather than what we hear; our eyes interfere with what we hear, even if our conscious brain knows about the McGurk effect. This is relevant, as all 'speech perception is inherently multimodal' (Rosenblum 2008, 405).

Although multimodal input can be used to disorientate, its main use is of course to enhance learning and memory retention. As discussed in the previous section, visual input plays an important role in retention and comprehension, and conversations are enhanced by the use of visual aids. There is also research to suggest meaningful gestures that accompany speech can enhance the comprehension of verbal messages (Wagner et al. 2014; Hostetter 2011). Particularly interesting, however, is the neurological effect of multimodal input. In an overview of current research, it was reported that subjects repeatedly performed better on recall tasks when multimodal formats were used compared to unimodal formats. It is easier to recall information that was learned multimodally as there are automatic connections made between verbal and visual information (Mastroberardino et al. 2008, 75).

In this way, there is a great deal of evidence to suggest that using augmented communication is likely to result in longer retention, more focused attention, and more convincing discussions in face-to-face communication. In addition, this only adds to the digital divide by adding a layer of embodied capital, what Bourdieu (1977) referred to as *habitus*, to these interactions. By this, I mean that in societies with high levels of digital integration, the digital divide is now moving into sociological realms involving face-to-face speech. Those who are not adept at using digital devices to augment their communication, or those who do not possess such devices for whatever reasons, may therefore be more likely to fall in the gap of the digital divide, as with people in lower-technology cultures.

Whilst it has already been acknowledged that mobile media could be exacerbating the digital divide, clearly the main people left behind are those in poorer regions with less access to technology, and this divide is deepening (van Dijk and van Deursen 2014). However, people from more developed nations could also fall into the divide if they do not have access, do not learn to use or otherwise resist the use of technology

(Goggin and Hjorth 2014). A 2009 study commissioned by UK mobile phone provider, TalkTalk, found that there were widely different levels of uptake and usage of digital technology, with the heavy users, so called 'digital extroverts' making up the second smallest of the six identified user-types (Zeitlyn 2009). This digital divide could end up having an influence on interpersonal and face-to-face interactions in the future, if augmented communication were to become widespread throughout developed societies.

Another aspect of this digital divide could also be the way people have access to certain types of information, which is another form of augmented communication, to which this discussion now turns.

5.2   INSTANT ACCESS TO KNOWLEDGE: EXOMEMORY

When asked by a reporter in Boston about the speed of sound, Einstein was being subjected to a pop quiz popular at the time due to the controversy surrounding the Edison test. Einstein famously replied 'I do not carry such information in my mind since it is readily available in books'. This quote has gone on to become an internet meme, often used to promote the idea that rote-learning of certain facts is unnecessary. Whilst Einstein certainly intended his comments to disparage the memorisation of statistics and espouse the purpose of education to 'train the mind to think' (Frank 1947, 185), this section asks the question as to whether or not augmented communication is making us 'smarter' or 'dumber' in terms of working memory and cognitive involvement.

As the Einstein story shows us, the fear that our population is 'getting dumber' or being 'dumbed down' is certainly not new. According to one of Einstein's biographies, the aforementioned Edison test was devised by the inventor Thomas Edison, who was getting 'crankier' with age. He had devised a set of job interview questions which featured items of a practical nature. Edison created this test because he 'disparaged American colleges as too theoretical' (Isaacson 2007, 299), and basically felt that people were not practical enough. Many well-educated people, including Edison's own son who had a degree from MIT, failed the 150 question test.

Neil Postman (2011) points out that in Plato's story *Phaedrus*, Thamus exhibits scepticism about the new technology of the written word, stating that it will make people more forgetful and lead to people being knowledgeable whilst remaining ignorant. Postman's book

Technopolis, like Carr (2010) and several others, make the case that modern technology, and especially the internet, are making us dumber. Like books, augmented communication further reduces the need for memorisation of facts, as information can be searched instantly and on the fly. Although I referred to this previously as augmented cognition, the main fear is about what is happening *inside* our heads, rather than how we use these networked tools in furtherance of the expanded mind.

It has been argued that this reconfiguration of mental processing skills is likely to have a profound effect on our minds, especially considering the plasticity of the brain and the ease with which cognitive functions can be re-wired, or 'evolution on the fly' as Calvin (1997) refers to it. As I have already stated, humans naturally use 'and exploit nonbiological props and scaffoldings' in order to further their present range of mental abilities (Clark 2003, 6). Thompson (2013) also presents a convincing case for this, providing various arguments for augmented cognition and listing examples which I have previously referred to as exomemory.

However, even if we can concur that utilising exomemory expands the limits of our own cognition, doing so only further implicates the need-to-find reliable sources of information, and thus to apply critical appraisals of information during such ad hoc learning situations.

5.2.1 The Speaker and the Search Engine

This section provides a discussion about how speakers do not necessarily need much prior knowledge to begin speaking on a subject if they are able to use their phones whilst simultaneously holding a conversation. This form of augmented cognition relies on exomemory being applied to fill knowledge gaps in a conversation or learn on the fly in order to continue a conversation. I also examine how this implicates working memory.

In an episode of the US sit-com *Friends*, Ross invites the boyfriend of his friend Phoebe, Mike, to his house in order to get to know him better. The episode's humour comes from the fact that the two men rapidly run out of things to talk about, and the evening becomes awkward. At one point, whist drinking a beer, Ross explains to Mike that what they are drinking is actually lager. Mike asks, 'what's the difference?', to which Ross replies that he doesn't know. It is only much later, after Mike has left and returned in order to distract Ross, that the pair resort to checking the difference in a dictionary. Had this episode been made within the last few years, the most natural thing to do would have been to pull out a smartphone and search the answer to the lager vs beer question as the conversation was in progress, thus facilitating and enhancing an existing practice (of looking things up during a conversation). I have made numerous ethnographic observations of this ad hoc searching, and I believe it to be one of the most widespread reasons for augmented communication.

Access to information has always been a form of social capital. John Field notes that 'social capital contributes to collective action by [...] facilitating flows of information' which allow people to make evaluative judgements about people in a network (Field 2008, 34). When people engage in augmented communication, they have access to extended networks of information or exomemory, and these can be almost seamlessly integrated into face-to-face communication in real time. Not only do search engines such as Google provide access to a vast repository of online information, there are also social networking sites such as Facebook and Twitter that further expand a person's access to information as a form of social capital, in the form of online shared memories or personal images or information about networked friends and their connections.

During face-to-face conversations, a speaker might mention something unfamiliar to the listener. The listener can simultaneously listen to the conversation whilst searching online for a basic explanation, picture or example. As this happens, the speaker may also use their phone to search for a more specific piece of information about the topic. If the topic under discussion is particularly current, it may be trending on SNS and thus a larger network of people could potentially be incorporated into the discussion.

Such interactions are taking place naturally in a variety of business and personal contexts in nations with high smartphone penetration. Engaging in these types of highly augmented conversations requires a certain set of skills and prerequisites, and with these come further complications and questions that researchers must ask themselves in order to understand the implications of such discourse patterns.

First, it is important to note the requirement of multitasking. Due to humans' limited cognitive capacities for real-time tasks and language parsing, multitasking is a skill that taps into the finite resource of working memory. Although it is possible to have a conversation whilst engaging in other activities, the more complex the activity the less focus can be assigned to the conversation. Eating and drinking are relatively undemanding tasks which generally do not impede on the quality of a conversation, whereas doing a crossword puzzle might entail that a person is unable to properly listen and participate in an ongoing conversation. The act of searching online requires the user to access the right apps, write in key search terms and then read the results, making judgements about which site to connect to for information. This is cognitively demanding and thus it seems unlikely that a person can fully search online during face-to-face conversation without some loss of attention (although, see the work of Jones 2005, 2010 for a discussion of 'attention structures' which view attention as a social activity). This becomes a blended form of digital literacy, and it entails its own set of sub-skills (Jenkins et al. 2013).

If this is the case, then why do people engage in online searches as part of face-to-face conversations? One reason is that people may mutually arrive at a topic about which neither speaker is fully sure, and thus the search becomes a form of checking information, which is also a collaborative activity; a co-construction of knowledge and part of their engagement with each other. This can be seen in my earlier example about Chiyori-san, where friends used a phone to search for a mutual friend in order to find out more about her since they had lost touch. The example from the episode of *Friends* illustrates how much conversations may have changed in the past two decades or so. It is perhaps less common for a person to search online when the person with whom they are speaking can just tell them what they need to know about a topic, however it is more likely when neither of the interlocutors feels fully confident about the topic. As previously touched upon, this strategy has been criticised as it could be seen to be a disconnect from the conversation in hand (see Sect. 4.3.2).

The act of searching online, being now such a common activity, becomes the focus of the conversation and leads to new directions of discourse. An obvious problem with this, however, is the choice of information and the trustworthiness of the source. In this way, people are talking about things and forming opinions whilst basically learning about the topic at the same time. If people do not exercise critical thought when selecting information, this could lead to serious issues later on, as I will discuss later in this chapter.

Another reason that people may use searches during face-to-face communication is as a form of note-taking or visual stimulus. One example I previously discussed was during my visit to Kyushu in Japan, when a person I had just met asked me to recommend some films to watch. As I listed each film, she opened a new tab on the Internet Movie Database (IMDB) site and kept the tabs open, presumably to look at more closely at a later time. This was a digital form of note-taking. In addition to the record on her phone, the visual of the picture and the actual act of conducting the search are likely to help commit the films to memory as well. An additional reason for searching might also be that people may feel they are losing face if a person begins to talk about an unfamiliar topic. By searching the topic themselves, a person is able to save face and gain an even footing, albeit an ad hoc one.

Returning to Einstein and the Edison Test, educational models in many developed nations have de-emphasised rote-learning and the memorisation of facts. One reason is that such information is 'readily available' at the touch of a touchscreen, in other words exomemory. However, does this mean that people are using their brains less and thus becoming less intelligent? Are smartphones making people dumb?

5.2.2   Getting Dumber Whilst Multitasking: Working Memory or New Literacies?

This section addresses the way face-to-face conversations with augmented communication now require multitasking skills which implies that fewer cognitive resources are devoted to the act of speaking yet overall more cognitive resources are used due to multitasking and possibly maintaining several conversations at once. This skill requires new types of literacies, and this is already being highlighted through discussions about the polymediated age (Herbig et al. 2015). Other scholars have discussed the fact that we are 'always on' and in constant connection (Baron 2008), and the way language and social media interact in ways that affect identity and community (Seargeant and Tagg 2014).

It has always been common to hear older generations bemoaning 'the youth of today' for either not being as smart or not having to work as hard. A quote falsely attributed to Socrates about how 'children love luxury' and 'show disrespect for elders' has been widely shared in order to make the point that each generation has cast its sceptical eye over the successors.[1] A clear example of this is the question of whether the UK's O-level high-school examinations were harder than modern GCSEs. British newspapers like *The Telegraph, The Guardian* and of course *The*

Daily Mail all have articles comparing these two examinations, many of them using real-life examples and inviting readers to answer the questions. But, could smartphones actually be causing this mass 'dumbing down' of society? It is now a common gag to say that smartphones are making dumb people, but is it really true?

There are examples of people getting into rather foolish accidents as a result of them being on their phones. In 2016 the *Pokémon Go* game caused a spate of accidents around the world. In Japan there was at least one fatal accident caused by a driver playing the game whilst behind the wheel. 36-year-old truck driver Nobusuke Kawai hit and killed 9-year-old Keita Noritake who was crossing the road at a pedestrian crossing in Ichinomiya on 26 October 2016. Kawai admitted to police that he had been playing the game whilst driving. In the US, over 110,000 road accidents were linked to the game by September 2016, just two months after its release in July. However, it is very difficult to say whether these people are 'stupid' or whether their phones made them 'stupid', especially as simply having a car crash is by no way an indicator of low intelligence. And yet, *The New York Times* did report that 2016 had seen the biggest spike in traffic accidents in 50 years, which was blamed primarily on apps being used on mobile phones (Boudette 2016). This seems to be an example of technological determinism, an emotive subject which is entwined also with discussions about the effect of technology on face-to-face interactions.

The main concern about smartphones making us dumber usually takes the form of the argument presented above, with examples of people doing 'stupid' or even dangerous things. Despite the existence of a large amount of anecdotal evidence, this argument cannot have a scientific conclusion as it falsely equates having accidents with having low intelligence. History is full of foolish mistakes, yet there may well be a link between technology use and dangerous driving. Here, it is important to remember that the fault is not with the technology per se, but with the person using it whilst their attention should be on other things.

One conclusion could be that people are more easily distracted, and finding themselves addicted to their digital devices. However, the majority of people realise that playing a computer game whilst driving is likely to cause a serious accident, and laws are already in place in many countries that prohibit phone usage whilst driving.

Although the arguments falsely equate certain behaviours utilising technology with falling intelligence, rather than getting dumber, it may just be that people are now developing new skills and improving other areas of intelligence. It would be fruitful to see if people are now better at multitasking or if they are quicker at reading, finding a conclusion and making a critical decision based on information they have just found online. As oppose to getting dumber, it might be that people are just developing different types of intelligence.

5.2.2.1 Working Memory

As touched upon in the previous section, a common criticism of smartphones is that they are making people dumber. Whilst I would argue that this is not necessarily the case, as other types of intelligence may just be being prioritised, there is still a serious issue with our use of smartphones. Whilst it may not be the case that we are actually getting dumber, the real danger may be more insidious than this, and linked to the Einstein quote used to start this section. The main worry could be to do with *working memory*.

Working memory is related to short-term memory, and was first proposed by Baddeley and Hitch (1974). Working memory is basically the brain's capacity to focus attention on immediate tasks. When a person walks into a room and realises that they have forgotten why they came in there, this is an example of working memory having failed. Games like the card game Snap, where players flip over a card and have to remember where the card's double is located, are tests of working memory. It is possible to exhaust working memory as it is a limited resource, but it is also possible to train working memory like a muscle in order to improve it. Working memory is also linked to cognitive load and peak attention, both of which have important implications for learning. In order to pass into longer-term memory, things have to pass through working memory first. A number of articles and research studies have recently reported that smartphones could be damaging users' working memory because they are 'quickly becoming an extension of the human brain' (Krauss Whitbourne 2011).

An example of how this becomes reality is illustrated in the following vignette. When I first met my wife, one of the things we had in common was a love of films. We often had conversations along the lines of 'who was the actress in *Amelie?*' to which one of us would reply 'Audrey Tattou' after a short thoughtful pause. As our brains retrieve this information, we are ensuring it stays in our minds for longer by re-accessing it. The process of information retrieval itself also strengthens connections in the brain. Nowadays, my wife and I tend to default to the IMDB app, which lists actors and actresses and the films they have worked on. When trying to remember what film we have seen a certain actor or actress, using IMDB now reduces the amount of cognitive load we are using, which it could be argued, is making us 'dumber'. However, the app's presence usually means that we find new films that we want to watch, an example of how the conversation takes a new direction as a result of augmented communication.

A study by Maguire et al. (2003) found that London taxi drivers, who spend three years learning their way around London in order to become registered black cab drivers, have an enlarged hippocampus compared to the general population, meaning that areas of their brain used for navigation had extended through usage. Needless to say, GPS and satellite navigation systems might undermine this type of brain training, possibly resulting in a less agile mind. My father has complained that since he started using GPS to find his way around, he no longer remembers the way and continually relies on the GPS to find his way back.

On the other hand, there are studies that have shown that playing computer games can improve attention, decision making speed and task performance (Svoboda and Richards 2009). Other research has shown that mobile learning or mLearning, can be utilised in order to develop a number of skills including foreign languages and mathematics (Goggin and Hjorth 2014; Cavus and Ibrahim 2009). In several countries, such as parts of the US, UK and Europe, iPads are given to school students with a range of educational apps and useful resources. The internet is an amazing resource for learning and accessing information, so whilst there is scientific evidence that some smartphone related practices could lead to an impairment of working memory, there is an equally valid argument that digital devices can also develop our brains and thinking capacity. Certainly, there seems to be an increase in types of multitasking behaviour during instant messaging conversations, as shown in a brief study by Baron (2008, 40–42). However, much more research is needed before firm conclusions can be drawn, although Baron later states that 'multitasking will be the nine-hundred-pound gorilla challenging users of language and communication technologies' (2008, 218), and she cites several neurological studies that demonstrate humans' limited capacity for multitasking, especially if we are interrupted during a task.

However, the crucial point here is that, rather than getting 'dumber', perhaps what digital technologies are facilitating is a shift in how we use our brains and what types of intelligence are needed to perform a new range of daily mental activities. Searching the internet, deciding what piques our interest, scanning the content and making judgements about it could all be seen as types of intelligence, but the vast amount of information available to us through these devices requires, perhaps now more than ever, a greater capacity for critical thinking.

5.3   CRITICAL THINKING AND THOUGHT CONTAGION

Critical thinking is a term often used to refer to an individual's ability to make informed and morally right decisions by weighing up different sides of an argument (King and Kitchener 1994). Such thought is highly prized in many societies and generally encouraged by liberal or democratic governments, which is thus reflected in educational policy. However, the sources we use to get information are rarely impartial, and yet newspapers and other media present themselves as factual, making it hard to resist their arguments. Building on the previous arguments, this section discusses the fact that many newspapers and publishers have their own agenda and that relying on the internet as a source of information during face-to-face communication seriously impairs the individuals' time for reflection and critical appraisal of the source.

Towards the end of 2016 there was a surge in news articles reporting the existence of 'fake news', a phenomena related to websites that claim to be legitimate news providers, but the stories are in fact completely fictitious and written with an agenda, usually one aimed at spreading fear, hatred or anger. The scale of fake news was such that in the UK, the Digital, Culture, Media and Sport (DCMS) Committee began an enquiry in 2017 (Seargeant and Tagg 2018). The 'fake news' story became a globally reported issue after an incident on 4 December 2016, in which Edgar Maddison Welch opened fire in a pizza restaurant in Washington, DC, having been led to believe there was a child sex ring being operated from the venue by then US presidential candidate, Hilary Clinton. Commenting on this event, Clinton denounced the 'epidemic' of fake news stating that it had 'real world consequences' (Gambino 2016).

The irony of course is that many of the newspapers that widely reported on the phenomena of fake news have themselves been criticised for biased reporting and for playing a role in the manipulation of the general public. Generally, people often look at their phones when they are between other tasks, for example on a commuter train or whilst waiting in line for their turn. At these times, people are likely to scroll through social media which contain a myriad of links to news stories.

Choosing to read one of these stories is based on the story having stood out to us and piqued our interest against a cacophony of other competing articles. As such, headlines are written using emotive language, often rephrased as a cliff-hanger or need-to-know statement such as '10 things you need to know to make your sex life hotter'. This practice is known collectively as 'click baiting', and in using emotive and leading language in such a way they may be more persuasive than other articles which take a more balanced view. Whilst between tasks, readers of such articles are unlikely to have their critical guard up, so to speak, and therefore may be unduly influenced by what they read, although this is mere conjecture at this point. Baron (2010) has made an important and convincing case that the language we use online has an impact in the way language evolves offline, and hence such click baiting is likely to take hold in face-to-face conversations, with the added power of augmented communication to enhance the impact of the message.

This is especially problematic when we consider that many large media companies are controlled by a small number of individuals, all of whom have their own political and social agendas. It has frequently been claimed that newspapers are able to swing elections in Britain, and evidence from a YouGov survey in the UK backs this up (Greenslade 2015). Writing in *The Guardian*, Greenslade traces the political alignments of various newspapers, yet he concludes that newspapers probably do not have as much influence as they themselves claim, partially due to the advent of televised debates. With newspapers in the UK having a long history of political alliance, readers will tend to choose the paper based on their political perspectives, rather than having their alignment swayed by the paper as they read, which is a form of confirmation bias (Oswald and Grosjean 2004). However, the power of the press to influence political results should not be underestimated. In light of the potentially more persuasive power of augmented communication, perhaps we should consider the power of those who control the media to shape political landscapes and the dangers of such individuals in light of new forms of communication that heavily rely on widely disseminated and ideologically biased forms of knowledge.

Rupert Murdoch, Haim Saban and Silvio Berlusconi are all so-called Media Moguls who own a disproportionate share of media networks in both printed and broadcast formats. Such people are able to command a great deal of influence in politics and business because of the way they can influence the public images of important issues and present facts about certain individuals. Levendusky (2013) has shown that partisan media is potentially polarising political opinions in the US, with many viewers tuning into channels that seem to only more deeply embed their biased beliefs. Confirmation bias is the tendency to search for, interpret and remember information in a way that makes it difficult for us to reject the hypothesis or alter our way of thinking (Oswald and Grosjean 2004). This is a very dangerous phenomenon, especially when linked to concepts such as *thought contagion* (Lynch 1996) and the spread of memes. Thought contagion basically posits that ideas and thoughts can spread quickly through groups in much the same way as epidemics. As a result, people can rapidly take on new ideas because of the power of a group, rather than taking the time to critically appraise and truly internalise the new values. A similar concept is emotional contagion, which explains how panic and hysteria can spread through empathic connections between large groups of individuals (Hatfield et al. 1993).

Despite this, there are governing bodies that offer strict guidelines for the way broadcasters can report on stories, and the sort of stories they can report on. Newspapers and television broadcasts are sometimes utilised by the police to help with criminal investigations, and state-funded services, like the BBC and NHK in Japan, are generally consistent at trying to present impartial news, although there are notable cases where this is not adhered to.

According to research compiled by inbound marketing and sales company, HubSpot, 71% of people are more likely to make a purchase if referred by social media (Ewing 2012). This implicates SNSs as powerful tools for forming and even manipulating opinions. The so-called Media Moguls are often portrayed as puppet masters who 'control the news' and with it they swing people's opinions and influence elections. The reality is that people often choose to read articles and seek evidence based on what they already believe (Hunt et al. 2016). Thus, although it is certainly true that newspapers can exert an influence on their readers, and that many news networks are monopolised by people with their own agendas, overestimating this influence fails to correctly take into account the individuals' personal agency at having selected the sources of their information. Clearly, education plays a crucial role in developing people's critical awareness, and ensuring people are capable of making their own informed choices about the decisions they are making.

5.4   SMARTPHONES ARE MAKING US DUMB (AND RUDE): ETIQUETTE AND COGNITIVE FUNCTIONS

No discussion of the impact of mobile phone and digital device usage would be complete without a discussion of etiquette. The negative aspects of mobile phone usage upon face-to-face communication are what mainly find their way into mainstream discussions. The issues under examination in this section have already been touched upon several times in previous ones, having cropped up continuously throughout the book. However, a short summary here seems appropriate, albeit this time from a slightly different perspective.

5.4.1   *Power, Politeness and Etiquette*

One regular criticism of smartphone usage during face-to-face interactions is that looking at a phone when another person is present could be seen as impolite, and there are numerous things we can do in such situations that might be considered bad etiquette. During the workgroup lessons mentioned in the methodology section, in which I discussed augmented communication with my students at a Japanese university, the overall attitude to the topic of smartphones and face-to-face interactions generally started off with a negative orientation. My students tended to believe that I would be approaching the topic from a negative point of view, and even after I had explained my research and the idea of augmented communication, many of them retained a cautionary approach to the use of smartphones during talk. This is likely to be due to the generally negative presentation of smartphone addiction in the Japanese media (Schreiber 2018); it is a common theme in English speaking countries too, that phones are 'ruining the art of conversation'.

These discussions generally focus on younger people, and as such they highlight some kind of 'generation gap' between those of us who do not use our phones and can still have a conversation, and the younger generation who are relying too much on texting and thus becoming less proficient in the 'art of conversation'. There are serious implications here, and the work of Sherry Turkle in looking into this area in particular is very convincing and provides excellent ethnographic observations into this phenomenon. And yet, there are several issues I would like to address in positing the arguments in these terms. First, it assumes that it is really only young people who are in danger, and that these trends are damaging in the first place. Secondly, the criticisms, especially those from less rigorous academic sources such as blogs and journalistic pieces, tend to assume that there is a set of rules to conversation, that people can be good or bad at holding conversations, implying there is a right and wrong way of going about talking to people in face-to-face exchanges. I will address each of these assumptions in turn.

In Sect. 4.2.2 when talking about apps, I mentioned Turkle's observations of a group in Boston who were using WhatsApp to augment their communication. What Turkle calls the 'Goldilocks effect' could also be equated with what Kozinets (2015) calls *consociation*.

> Rather than the tight bonds of community, an important form of contact guiding human relations in contemporary society seems to be consociation. We can think of consociation as a commonplace, largely instrumental, and often incidental form of association, one that we often take for granted because it has become so natural. (Kozinets 2015, 11)

Kozinets states that this lesser form of friendly yet ultimately shallow form of friendship is temporary, bounded and yet affable. In my view, this view of human relationships is pragmatic, and likely a product of the unprecedentedly large global population, and subsequent expanded social networks which characterise a global society of multicultural and highly mobile people.

First, as my own data has shown, it is not only young people who use their phones for conversation. It is therefore, not only young people who need to be aware of how using phones during social interaction can affect conversation, or who need to be aware of issues of politeness and etiquette. Focusing on the generational aspect serves to highlight issues of power which are implicated in discussions of politeness. The previous observation from the Japanese bathhouse (Sect. 4.1.1) is an interesting example as it shows that older people use their smartphones in the same way to do augmented communication, and as this example clearly shows, the function here it to build connectedness and enhance the conversation multimodally. As the examples in Vignette Four showed, older generations are also using their phones in face-to-face conversations.

Next I will address the observation that younger generations prefer texting to talking, that there is 'a communication divide, of sorts [between the talkers vs. the texters]' (Associated Press 2012). Around twenty years ago, Baron (1998) was already discussing the impact of email on conversation, and she concluded that written language was taking on the forms of spoken dialogue. She described this as 'speech by other means'. As Tagg (2015) points out, applied linguists have moved on from discussing online language use as either a form of written or spoken discourse, and rather the tendency is now to view it from its own multifaceted framework.

However, I must also exercise caution when discussing this issue, as my data concerning younger adults tends to be with 18–22-year-old Japanese university students, and thus it would be unwise to generalise or to compare my findings with those of Turkle (2012, 2015a, b), whose data set comes from the US and represents a broader age-group for young people.

According to Norman Fairclough, politeness 'is based upon recognition of differences of power, degrees of social distance, and so forth, and oriented to reproducing them without change' (2001, 55). Politeness is implicit when we negotiate social situations that feature an element of power imbalance (Harris 2007). Such encounters are actually extremely common, as we can observe in exchanges as simple as those between, say, a doctor and patient, a teacher and a student, a boss and an employee and so on. An essential aspect to politeness is the maintenance of one's face.

As I mentioned during Vignette Two, when my father began playing ringtones to me in an otherwise fairly quiet pub, I became embarrassed as I worried the noise might irritate other patrons. When mobile phones were just beginning to become more widely diffused, a study in Italy found that the dominant emotion that people had towards them was one of embarrassment (Vincent and Fortunati 2014).

Etiquette is such an important consideration in relation to online and digital forms of communication that it even has its own term: netiquette. However, for augmented communication we are not concerned with netiquette vs etiquette, as clearly in this context the two are once again united. Many people I spoke to would originally say that they felt negatively about the use of mobile phones during face-to-face interactions. It is only after explaining that I am examining situations where the phone is a natural part of the conversations that people tend to realise that mobile devices do not automatically exclude other interlocutors who are present in physical and temporal space. In other words, the general initial reaction to phones and face-to-face conversation is that they are incompatible. It seems that this is a reaction likely to have been born from experience (and coloured by the discussions surrounding it), as I imagine many people have encountered situations where someone with whom we are trying to have a conversation snubs them in favour of their phone. During a job interview in February 2017, I felt a great loss of confidence because the head of department was looking at his phone during my introduction. And, of course, the shoe can be on the other foot, when we are in situations where we find ourselves losing interest in the conversation around us, the interactions we could be having on our phone may seem more appealing.

This is certainly something I have heard in reports from my own workgroup lesson students, who helped me collect observations through systematic self-observation. During a class on 4 October 2017 with my linguistics seminar, one student, Tuck, told me that he often looked at his phone during face-to-face interactions. He explained though, that at first he had thought that he was 'just bored with the conversation', but after conducting a deeper reflection through the observation task I had set in the class, he realised that it was actually more complex than this. He continued that he had realised what he was actually doing was look-ing for new topics to turn the conversation away from the 'boring' topic and onto something he found more interesting. In some ways, this is the augmented communication version of channel surfing. Other students in the group admitted to doing similar things, although in general this was still viewed as bad etiquette.

At other times, however, the withdrawal from the face-to-face inter-action is not an attempt to salvage a conversation or find more interest-ing topics to discuss. It is a withdrawal of intent, something which could even be labelled as a passive act of resistance. This is the cause for many of the arguments between parents and teenagers. According to a report by Common Sense Media (2016), 36% of parents argue daily with their children about smartphone usage.

This brings me to some interesting observations that I made whilst in Argentina in September 2017. It was my first time to visit the country, and subsequently nearly everyone I met was someone I was meeting for the first time. Many of these people had made contact prior to meeting me, in order to arrange things, and I had already become close friends with one person through our regular online interactions over SNS over a period of a few years. However, one thing that I did find very interesting was the difference in etiquette involving mobile phones which I perceived.

In Japan, smartphones are extremely popular, although they are often demonised in the media. The issue of 'dumbwalking' is a serious problem in Japan, although in Japanese it is known as *arukinagara* (walking whilst [on the phone]). In particular, it can cause accidents at train stations, and congestion in an already overcrowded city, which has led to an influx of new warning signs over the past few years.

Other examples of the negative media reports on smartphone include the *sumahobusu* or ugly-face caused by smartphone (Fig. 5.1).

This image comes from an unknown Japanese TV show especially aimed at women, which warns that looking down and frowning constantly at your smartphone can make you less attractive. It seems that the media is happy to blame smartphones for almost anything.

Japanese culture is well-known to have particularly complex etiquette rules, with forms of politeness actually being built into the language. In Japanese, verbs are conjugated differently to make them more polite with the suffix -masu, and sometimes completely different words and

Fig. 5.1 Sumahobusu

structures are used, as in with *keigo* which is a form of formal speech in Japan. Travelling from Japan to Argentina is perhaps why I noticed these particular differences relating to etiquette. One of the things I found most striking was that the people I met in Argentina reported trying to be understanding about the fact that we are a*lways on* (Baron 2008). By this I mean that many of the people I met in Argentina (who were nearly all teachers themselves) try to be flexible and understanding towards their students about that fact that sometimes their personal lives will intersect with classroom time in the form of emergency texts and messages. In Argentina, by far the most popular app used for communication is WhatsApp, which allows the transmission of SMS messages and audio files, and live video and audio chats are also possible.

One of my new friends, Mercedes, who lives in Buenos Aires and works as a language teacher and teacher trainer, told me that phones are technically banned because most schools have a strict policy prohibiting students from using them in class. However, she has overruled this, and allows her students to check facts on their phones, and even look at messages, if they are important. Another colleague, Griselda, told me that sometimes her daughter calls during classes (when she is actually teaching), and she explains to the class that it's her daughter and puts her on speakerphone to say hello to the class. If the call is not important, the daughter says hi and tells her mother the nature of the call (we are out of milk, for example), but if the call is serious then the daughter might ask to be taken off speakerphone. Mercedes also told me that her elderly mother calls every evening at seven, just to let her know that she is ok. Sometimes, Mercedes is teaching at this time and cannot answer, but she lets the phone ring and her students are aware that it will ring at seven, but they also know the reason. From these observations and my short time in Argentina, I noticed that phone etiquette very much revolved around explaining the context of any incoming calls or phone usage. 'It's my mother, she's just come back from the hospital'. 'It's my daughter, she is getting her exam results today'. Or, for instance someone needs to quickly text another party to coordinate a meeting which is unfurling at that moment.

In this way, the 'emergency' call is not perhaps an accurate description, but there are always calls or usages which seem to take precedence at that moment over face-to-face interactions. Also, perhaps due to this more flexible attitude to phone etiquette during classes, it seems that people sometimes check their messages during classes, and then bring others around them into the message in order to make it acceptable etiquette. In the following example, my friend Darío was conducting a teacher education lesson with future teachers when I messaged him at 20:09 from Ezeiza International Airport in Buenos Aires to tell him that my plane had been delayed by 24 hours. I did not know that he was teaching a class, and it never occurred to me that he would check his messages if he were busy or otherwise engaged. He replied under 10 minutes later with a cheerful selfie with his 'loving future colleagues'. He later explained that he turned his class discussion around to me and the nature of my visit. Including me and his students together in the message widened our sense of community. Even though I have never met these future colleagues of Darío's, if I ever do we have already shared this moment.

I find this to be in contrast with other cultures, such as in the UK, where students may even have to hand in their phones at the start of class, where they are kept in a locked desk. This also happens in Argentina too, where high-school students are not allowed to look at their phones and are likely to have them confiscated. But, in Darío's class, where the students were other adults about to become teachers, such measures were not deemed necessary, and the issue of etiquette is overcome by involving all the people in the room in the personal communication. Despite this more flexible attitude to phones in Argentina, during academic presentations I never heard any phones and I did not see any behaviour I would class as 'rude' during more formal public events.

What these observations show is that the issue of etiquette (and netiquette) are very fluid and as strategies of discourse change and evolve, so too do the rules of etiquette surrounding them. In terms of augmented communication, although there is a great deal of suspicion, resentment and trepidation about the way mobile digital devices are affecting face-to-face communication, there are also times when using our phones as part of the conversation is acceptable, and when checking our messages even when they are not part of the immediate conversation can be done politely without causing a loss of face or insulting the other party.

But, being rude is only one part of the argument against modern technology and its hold over our lives in today's 'always on' culture. A much deeper existential crisis is also at stake.

5.5   *DASEIN* OR 'BEING THERE': AUTHENTICITY
AND AUGMENTED COMMUNICATION

Drawing on existential questions about the depersonalising effect of technology, specifically by expanding on Heidegger's concept of Dasein, which is related to authenticity and identity, this section returns to the issue addressed at the start of the book; that many complaints are levelled at smartphones for ruining face-to-face communication and making people simultaneously connected but disconnected. This section discusses how people's communication is changing to reflect a society in which the once clear division between online and offline is rapidly fading, and how people live both online and offline simultaneously. Just as Baron (1998) identified almost 20 years ago that written text is in a form of transition due to ICT, it seems that spoken and verbal communication is also undergoing a transition through the use of augmented communication.

At my son's kindergarten in Tokyo, the handouts we receive at events where parents can attend, such as sports days and school plays, will nearly always have a note to parents prohibiting us from using our phones. The note reads 'don't watch through a lens, look with your own eyes [translated from Japanese]' (see Fig. 5.2).

Not only are smartphones and other mobile networked devices often criticised for damaging conversations and leading to poor etiquette, they are also criticised for causing an even deeper existential crisis. Figure 5.3 shows a photograph I took at the station near my work in 2016, which reads *Inochi to sumaho. Dochira ga taisetsu desuka?* [Life or smartphone. Which is more important?]. During one of my workgroup lessons on 11 October 2017, one of my students who had spent some time abroad in Canada, shared a photograph during class which she had taken of a blackboard outside a well-known café (see Fig. 5.4). The board advertised the fact that this café had 'NO Wifi', and decided to make this a selling point. The board read 'talk to each other. Call your mum' and 'Live!'. The implication here is that, with internet connections, we fail to make or maintain the important personal connections that comprise our 'real life'. In other words, the online world is fake, inauthentic, whereas the offline world is the real, authentic one. Whilst there could be some truth in such a view, framing it as such also misses the woods for the trees.

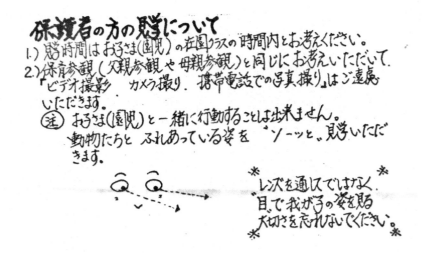

Fig. 5.2 Japanese kindergarten—look with your own eyes

In 2014, a YouTube video entitled *Look Up* by Gary Turk went viral. At the time of writing it has over 60 million views. It has even spawned a parody, entitled *Look Down*. The content of the *Look Up* video is a poem and a visual story of a man whose life goes in two directions because he either met a girl on the street to ask directions, or (in the alternative version) he was looking at his phone and presumably using GPS to navigate his way around. There are some very poignant parts to this video, and much of its message I can agree with. The basic premise is that we miss out of 'real' life by being too obsessed with the 'virtual' life, which we tend to access through networked mobile devices.

This video clearly struck a chord with the online community, causing it to be shared and viewed many times over, and yet ironically (as more than one YouTube commenter has also wryly noted) quite often this sharing would be taking place on smartphones. So, effectively people are using their phones and are quite aware of the anti-social implications, yet they continue to do so anyway.

As I have already shown, there are many claims levelled against technology destroying face-to-face conversations. Sherry Turkle, having spent her early career researching the digital or *Second Self* (2005), now believes technology is causing a withdrawal from authentic personal

Fig. 5.3   Life or smartphone

and meaningful relationships (2012), and warns that such a trend could impair the development of social and empathic skills in younger generations (2015a).

However, as I have discussed elsewhere in this book when examining the idea of networked publics (see Sect. 4.4.3), young people cannot simply separate their online and offline identities, and they constantly have to navigate through a networked world of context collapse online, with multiple identities being reconstructed as they try to understand the ever fluctuating norms of a polymediated age, or even a 'polyreality' (Dunn 2015). To this end, both Turkle and boyd share a similar view. As boyd explains, our priority should be to address the issues that are at the

Fig. 5.4 No Wifi as a selling point

crux of problematic behaviour, 'rather than propagate distracting myths. Fear is not the solution: empathy is' (2014, 127).

Expecting tomorrows' future generations to interact, socialise and converse in the same way that the previous generation did is like expecting those same generations to know how to operate a wireless radio (an exercise in futility that the BBC Radio 4's *Today Show* actually did on their Facebook page on 29 September 2017). Just as languages are ever evolving, so too are the societies that speak them.

It is easy to make technology the target of our hopes and anxieties. Newness makes it the perfect punching bag. But one of the hardest – and yet most important – things we as a society must think about in the face of technological change is what has really changed, and what has not. [...] It is much harder to examine the broad systematic changes with a critical lens and to place them in historical context than to focus on what is new and disruptive. (boyd 2014, 211–12)

In the BBC's attempt to highlight the 'youth of today's' inability to use a wireless, they reflect a mirror back on themselves as media, and our society's expectations of them. Do we want the next generation to be just like us? Are the previous generations really so successful, so superior in their overall ability to care for one another, to talk and to listen and to empathise with each other? Commenting on the BBC's street-level experiment, my friend pointed me in the direction of a quote from Jon Bois on Twitter (see quote below), which sarcastically and yet artfully highlights the backwards nature of such thinking.

these days it seems like people are always on their iphones instead of thatching roofs or following the edicts of edward the confessor
2:35 AM - 27 Sep 2017

The previously mentioned *Look Up* video is not an isolated example. In a blog post for the site *Blaze Press*, the author notes that:

Thanks to smartphones we have never been so connected to people that can be as far as the other side of the world, whilst being left feeling disconnected from those right next to us. These illustrations highlight how smartphones are causing the death of conversation and changing social interaction as we know it. (Blaze Press 2015)

This post, entitled *27 Powerful Images That Sum up How Smartphones Are Ruining Our Lives* has currently been shared 3.2 million times, and likely the images have found their way onto many more screens than this through other links and shares.

In the September 2017 issue of *The Atlantic*, Twenge (2017) asks if the smartphone has 'destroyed a generation'. Common Sense Media (2016) and its widely reproduced findings about smartphone addiction also contribute to a growing sense of panic that smartphones are inherently dangerous, dehumanising us and making us into 'zombies'.

Again, it is worth noting that all this negative press is merely one side of the story, and that whilst it is true that smartphone usage has been linked with feelings of isolation and anxiety, they are also being used in ways which do not 'kill conversations' or even disconnect us from 'reality', but rather quite the opposite. The vignettes and observations I have presented in this book thus far have all been heavily contextualised, in order to show the human aspects of augmented communication. In terms of connecting people and bringing people together, augmented communication is certainly not without its pitfalls, limitations, and even dangers. However, my observations have lead me to believe that many people are now employing their phones in naturally innovative ways as tools to enhance face-to-face conversations, just as they are employed to stay in touch with people in other parts of the world. The following comments from the previously mentioned Blaze Press post show how people are applying a critical mindset to the story of 'phones are ruining conversation'.

E. A. Christofferson

I completely disagree. Cell phones have allowed me to communicate with people about important and non important things at a moments notice. They choose to answer the phone or look at the text and respond. I have a map app on my phone and a notepad app that allows me to remember important things like sending flowers for Mother's Day. People have taken recordings of professionals acting in a most unprofessional way, allowing us to investigate acts of injustice. As with every new invention, we need to mature in our use of it but I honestly believe it has helped to improved society and our relationships with each other.

GK replying to E. A. Christofferson

This type of complaint is one of my biggest pet peeves. Smart phones connect us to each other and a wealth of information in a way we did not have a decade ago. The fact that there is a downside is not surprising. As with any advancement, we have to balance the good with the bad. I would argue that our lives are, on balance, enhanced by this technology. Choosing only to portray the downside as truth is an unfair incomplete picture that misleads those incapable of ration consideration.

R Peterson replying to GK

But I think most people realize the benefits of the technology and these comics are just illustrating those downsides. The artists aren't necessarily trying to show a complete argument of the pros and cons. They already understand that the technology is here to stay and that there are plenty of people lauding them. They're merely showing what happens when a good thing goes too far.

This shows how the authors of these comments see smartphones as potentially empowering devices that can be used for a number of functions, many of which benefit society and do not negatively impact on the user.

As I have previously and continuously stated, the reality is likely to lie somewhere in the middle. It is just as unhelpful to take one polarised side as it is that of another, but rather a descriptive, contextualised and level-headed examination is needed in order to fully understand the impact of digital devices on our societies, particularly their impact on face-to-face communication.

5.6   SUMMARY

In summary, this chapter has aimed to present the various aspects that make up the central argument that smartphones are making people 'less smart', or creating a broader existential crisis. The chapter discussed working memory, and pointed out that whilst working memory can be impaired by certain practices of use with digital devices, other types of intelligence can also be fostered. Thus, a shift in intelligence might be a more accurate observation rather than a general 'dumbing down'. Secondly, the way users access news stories on their phones was examined, and the possible dangers of this were discussed, alongside a broader argument that warned against neglecting the agency of each individual as they select sources for information. In short, augmented communication implies a change in the way many people communicate, which is likely to have a neurological impact. Due to the structure of mass media and the way we access information on the fly, I believe critical thinking skills have become an essential aspect of this new form of blended digital literacy.

5.6.1   Reflection

Readers are invited to assess the positionality of information sources and to observe the possible impact of such texts.

NOTE

1. The quote runs as follows: 'The children now love luxury. They have bad manners, contempt for authority; they show disrespect for elders and love chatter in place of exercise.' However, according to Garson O'Toole, this quote actually appears to come from a Cambridge student, Kenneth John Freeman's dissertation which was published in 1907. The quote has been attributed to Socrates and Plato in newspapers around the world since around 1922, and has become even more widely shared now on the internet. A full history of the misrepresentation of this quote can be found on the Quote Investigator site at http://quoteinvestigator.com/2010/05/01/misbehaving-children-in-ancient-times/.

REFERENCES

Apperson, Jennifer M., Eric L. Laws, and James A. Scepansky. 2006. "The Impact of Presentation Graphics on Students' Experience in the Classroom." *Computers & Education* 47 (1): 116–26. http://dx.doi.org/10.1016/j.compedu.2004.09.003.

Associated Press. 2012. "Is Texting Ruining the Art of Conversation? Fear We Are Losing Ability to Have Traditional Face-to-Face Conversations." *Daily News*. Accessed October 26. http://www.nydailynews.com/life-style/texting-ruining-art-conversation-fear-losing-ability-traditional-face-to-face-conversations-article-1.1089679.

Baddeley, Alan D., and Graham Hitch. 1974. "Working Memory." In *Psychology of Learning and Motivation*, edited by H. Bower Gordon, 47–89. New York: Academic Press.

Baron, Naomi S. 1998. "Letters by Phone or Speech by Other Means: The Linguistics of Email." *Language & Communication* 18 (2): 133–70. https://doi.org/10.1016/S0271-5309(98)00005-6.

Baron, Naomi S. 2008. *Always On: Language in an Online and Mobile World*. Oxford: Oxford University Press.

Baron, Naomi S. 2010. "Assessing the Internet's Impact on Language." In *The Handbook of Internet Studies*, edited by Robert Burnett, Mia Consalvo, and Charles Ess, 117–36. Sussex: Blackwell.

Bird, S. Elizabeth. 2011. "Are We All Produsers Now?: Convergence and Media Audience Practices." *Cultural Studies* 25 (4–5): 502–16. https://doi.org/10.1080/09502386.2011.600532.

Blaze Press. 2015. "27 Powerful Images That Sum Up How Smartphones Are Ruining Our Lives: The Death of Conversation." Blaze Press. Accessed October 29. https://blazepress.com/2015/05/27-powerful-images-that-sum-up-how-smartphones-are-ruining-our-lives/.

Boudette, Neal. 2016. "Biggest Spike in Traffic Deaths in 50 Years? Blame Apps." *The New York Times*, November 15, Business Day. Accessed February 15, 2017. https://www.nytimes.com/2016/11/16/business/tech-distractions-blamed-for-rise-in-traffic-fatalities.html?_r=0.

Bourdieu, Pierre. 1977. *Outline of a Theory of Practice*. Translated by Richard Nice. Cambridge: Cambridge University Press. Reprint, 2002.

Bourgeois, Michelle S. 1990. "Enhancing Conversation Skills in Patients with Alzheimer's Disease Using a Prosthetic Memory Aid." *Journal of Applied Behavior Analysis* 23 (1): 29–42. https://doi.org/10.1901/jaba.1990.23-29.

Bourgeois, Michelle S. 1993. "Effects of Memory Aids on the Dyadic Conversations of Individuals with Dementia." *Journal of Applied Behavior Analysis* 26 (1): 77–87. https://doi.org/10.1901/jaba.1993.26-77.

boyd, danah. 2014. *It's Complicated: The Social Lives of Networked Teens*. New Haven, CT: Yale University Press.

Calvin, William H. 1997. *How Brains Think: Evolving Intelligence, Then and Now*. London: Basic Books.

Carr, Nicholas. 2010. *The Shallows: What the Internet Is Doing to Our Brains*. New York, NY: W. W. Norton.

Cavus, Nadire, and Dogan Ibrahim. 2009. "m-Learning: An Experiment in Using SMS to Support Learning New English Language Words." *British Journal of Educational Technology* 40 (1): 78–91. https://doi.org/10.1111/j.1467-8535.2007.00801.x.

Clark, Andy. 2003. *Natural-Born Cyborgs: Minds, Technologies, and the Future of Human Intelligence*. New York: Oxford University Press.

Common Sense Media. 2016. *Technology Addiction: Concern, Controversy, and Finding Balance*. San Francisco, CA: Common Sense Media.

Drago, Emily. 2015. "The Effect of Technology on Face-to-Face Communication." *The Elon Journal of Undergraduate Research in Communications* 6 (1): 13–19.

Dunn, Robert Andrew. 2015. "Polyreality." In *Beyond New Media: Discourse and Critique in a Polymediated Age*, edited by Art Herbig, Andrew F. Herrmann, and Adam W. Tyma, 109–24. London: Lexington Books.

Ewing, Mike. 2012. "71% More Likely to Purchase Based on Social Media Referrals." *HubSpot*. Accessed February 21, 2017. https://blog.hubspot.com/blog/tabid/6307/bid/30239/71-More-Likely-to-Purchase-Based-on-Social-Media-Referrals-Infographic.aspx#sm.000o9nydesp5dq3106j22caz48wih.

Fairclough, Norman. 2001. *Language and Power (Language in Social Life)*, 2nd ed. Harlow: Longman.

Field, John. 2008. *Social Capital (Key Ideas)*, 2nd ed. London: Routledge.

Frank, Philipp. 1947. *Einstein: His Life and Times*. New York, NY: Alfred A. Knopf.

Gambino, Lauren. 2016. "Hillary Clinton Warns Fake News Can Have 'Real World Consequences'." *The Guardian*, December 9. Accessed February 15,

2017. https://www.theguardian.com/us-news/2016/dec/08/hillary-clinton-fake-news-consequences-pizzagate.

Glenberg, Arthur M., and William E. Langston. 1992. "Comprehension of Illustrated Text: Pictures Help to Build Mental Models." *Journal of Memory and Language* 31 (2): 129–51. http://dx.doi. org/10.1016/0749-596X(92)90008-L.

Goggin, Gerard, and Larissa Hjorth (eds.). 2014. *The Routledge Companion to Mobile Media*. London: Routledge.

Greenslade, Roy 2015. "Newspaper Readers' Election Votes Reveal Influence of Rightwing Press." *The Guardian*, June 8. https://www.theguardian. com/media/greenslade/2015/jun/08/newspaper-reader-election-ukip-express-sun-mail-telegraph.

Harris, Sandra. 2007. "Politeness and Power." In *The Routledge Companion to Sociolinguistics*, edited by Carmen Llamas, Louise Mullany, and Peter Stockwell, 122–29. London: Routledge.

Hatfield, Elaine, John T. Cacioppo, and Richard L. Rapson. 1993. "Emotional Contagion." *Current Directions in Psychological Science* 2 (3): 96–100. https://doi.org/10.1111/1467-8721.ep10770953.

Herbig, Art, Andrew F. Herrmann, and Adam W. Tyma (eds.). 2015. *Beyond New Media: Discourse and Critique in a Polymediated Age*. London: Lexington Books.

Hill, Andrea, Tammi Arford, Amy Lubitow, and Leandra M. Smollin. 2012. "I'm Ambivalent About It." *Teaching Sociology* 40 (3): 242–56. https://doi. org/10.1177/0092055x12444071.

Hostetter, Autumn B. 2011. "When Do Gestures Communicate? A Meta-Analysis." *Psychological Bulletin* 137 (2): 297.

Hunt, Laurence T., Robb B. Rutledge, W.M. Nishantha Malalasekera, Steven W. Kennerley, and Raymond J. Dolan. 2016. "Approach-Induced Biases in Human Information Sampling." *PLoS Biology* 14 (11): e2000638.

Isaacson, Walter. 2007. *Einstein: His Life and Universe*. New York: Simon & Schuster.

Jenkins, Henry, Sam Ford, and Joshua Green. 2013. *Spreadable Media: Creating Value and Meaning in a Networked Culture*. New York, NY: New York University Press.

Jones, Rodney H. 2005. "Sites of Engagement as Sites of Attention: Time, Space and Culture in Electronic Discourse." In *Discourse in Action: Introducing Mediated Discourse Analysis*, edited by Sigrid Norris and Rodney H. Jones, 141–54. London: Routledge.

Jones, Rodney H. 2010. "Cyberspace and Physical Space: Attention Structures in Computer Mediated Communication." In *Semiotic Landscapes: Text, Space and Globalization*, edited by A. Jaworski and C. Thurlow, 151–67. London: Continuum.

King, Patricia M., and Karen Strohm Kitchener. 1994. *Developing Reflective Judgment: Understanding and Promoting Intellectual Growth and Critical Thinking in Adolescents and Adults, Higher and Adult Education*. San Francisco, CA: Jossey-Bass.

Kozinets, Robert V. 2015. *Netnography: Redefined*, 2nd ed. London: Sage.

Krauss Whitbourne, Susan 2011. "Your Smartphone May Be Making You... Not Smart: Is the Latest iPhone Hazardous to Your Brain?" *Psychology Today*, October 18.

Lari, Fateme Samiei. 2014. "The Impact of Using PowerPoint Presentations on Students' Learning and Motivation in Secondary Schools." *Procedia— Social and Behavioral Sciences* 98: 1672–77. http://dx.doi.org/10.1016/j.sbspro.2014.03.592.

Levendusky, Matthew. 2013. *How Partisan Media Polarize America*. Chicago, IL: University of Chicago Press.

Lynch, Aaron. 1996. *Thought Contagion: How Belief Spreads Through Society*. New York: Basic Books.

Maguire, Eleanor A., Hugo J. Spiers, Catriona D. Good, Tom Hartley, Richard S. J. Frackowiak, and Neil Burgess. 2003. "Navigation Expertise and the Human Hippocampus: A Structural Brain Imaging Analysis." *Hippocampus* 13 (2): 250–59. https://doi.org/10.1002/hipo.10087.

Mastroberardino, Serena, Valerio Santangelo, Fabiano Botta, Francesco S. Marucci, and Marta Olivetti Belardinelli. 2008. "How the Bimodal Format of Presentation Affects Working Memory: An Overview." *Cognitive Processing* 9 (1): 69–76. https://doi.org/10.1007/s10339-007-0195-6.

Mayer, Richard E. 2002. "Multimedia Learning." In *Psychology of Learning and Motivation*, 85–139. San Diego, CA: Academic Press.

Mayer, Richard E., and Valerie K. Sims. 1994. "For Whom Is a Picture Worth a Thousand Words? Extensions of a Dual-Coding Theory of Multimedia Learning." *Journal of Educational Psychology* 86 (3): 389.

McGurk, Harry, and John MacDonald. 1976. "Hearing Lips and Seeing Voices." *Nature* 264: 746–48.

Michel, Jean-Baptiste, Yuan Kui Shen, Aviva Presser Aiden, Adrian Veres, Matthew K. Gray, Joseph P. Pickett, Dale Hoiberg, Dan Clancy, Peter Norvig, Jon Orwant, Steven Pinker, Martin A. Nowak, and Erez Lieberman Aiden. 2011. "Quantitative Analysis of Culture Using Millions of Digitized Books." *Science* 331 (6014): 176–82. https://doi.org/10.1126/science.1199644.

Oswald, Margit E., and Stefan Grosjean. 2004. "Confirmation Bias." In *Cognitive Illusions: A Handbook on Fallacies and Biases in Thinking, Judgement and Memory*, edited by Rüdiger F. Pohl, 79–96. New York, NY: Psychology Press.

OxfordDictionaries.com. 2013. "OxfordDictionaries.com August 2013 New Words Update." Accessed October 26, 2017. https://blog.oxforddictionaries.com/august-2013-update/.

Postman, Neil. 2011. *Technopoly: The Surrender of Culture to Technology*. London: Vintage.

Przybylski, Andrew K., and Netta Weinstein. 2013. "Can You Connect with Me Now? How the Presence of Mobile Communication Technology Influences Face-to-Face Conversation Quality." *Journal of Social and Personal Relationships* 30 (3): 237–46.

Rosenblum, Lawrence D. 2008. "Speech Perception as a Multimodal Phenomenon." *Current Directions in Psychological Science* 17 (6): 405–9.

Schreiber, Mark. 2018. "There's No Easy Way to Escape from Your Smartphone." *The Japan Times*, Last modified 4th August 2018. Accessed August 23. https://www.japantimes.co.jp/news/2018/08/04/national/media-national/theres-no-easy-way-escape-smartphone/#.W35DgOgza70.

Seargeant, Philip, and Caroline Tagg (eds.). 2014. *The Language of Social Media: Identity and Community on the Internet*. Basingstoke: Palgrave Macmillan.

Seargeant, Philip, and Caroline Tagg. 2018. "Fake News and Digital Literacy." Palgrave. Accessed August 23. https://www.palgrave.com/gb/social-science-matters/seargeant-and-tagg-on-fake-news-and-digital-literacy.

Smith, Rachel E. 2011. "Urban Dictionary: Youth Slanguage and the Redefining of Definition: What's Up with Meep and Other Words in the Urban Dictionary." *English Today* 27 (4): 43–48. https://doi.org/10.1017/s0266078411000526.

Svoboda, Eva, and Brian Richards. 2009. "Compensating for Anterograde Amnesia: A New Training Method That Capitalizes on Emerging Smartphone Technologies." *Journal of the International Neuropsychological Society* 15 (4): 629–38.

Tagg, Caroline. 2015. *Exploring Digital Communication: Language in Action*. London: Routledge.

Thompson, Clive. 2013. *Smarter Than You Think: How Technology Is Changing Our Minds for the Better*. New York, NY: Penguin.

Turkle, Sherry. 2005. *The Second Self: Computers and the Human Spirit*, 20th Anniversary ed. Cambridge, MA: MIT Press.

Turkle, Sherry. 2012. *Alone Together: Why We Expect More from Technology and Less from Each Other*. Philadelphia, PA: Basic books.

Turkle, Sherry. 2015a. *Reclaiming Conversation: The Power of Talk in a Digital Age*. New York: Penguin Press.

Turkle, Sherry. 2015b. "Stop Googling: Let's Talk." *The New York Times*, SR1. http://www.nytimes.com/2015/09/27/opinion/sunday/stop-googling-lets-talk.html.

Twenge, Jean M. 2017. "Have Smartphones Destroyed a Generation?" *The Atlantic*.

Ushioda, Ema. 2011. "Language Learning Motivation, Self and Identity: Current Theoretical Perspectives." *Computer Assisted Language Learning* 24 (3): 199–210. https://doi.org/10.1080/09588221.2010.538701.

van Dijk, Jan A.G.M., and Alexander J.A.M. van Deursen. 2014. *Digital Skills: Unlocking the Information Society.* Basingstoke: Palgrave Macmillan.

Vincent, Jane, and Leopoldina Fortunati. 2014. "The Emotional Identity of the Mobile Phone." In *The Routledge Companion to Mobile Media*, edited by Gerard Goggin and Larissa Hjorth, 312–19. London: Routledge.

Wade, Kimberley A., Maryanne Garry, Don J. Read, and D. Stephen Lindsay. 2002. "A Picture Is Worth a Thousand Lies: Using False Photographs to Create False Childhood Memories." *Psychonomic Bulletin & Review* 9 (3): 597–603. https://doi.org/10.3758/bf03196318.

Wagner, Petra, Zofia Malisz, and Stefan Kopp. 2014. "Gesture and Speech in Interaction: An Overview." *Speech Communication* 57: 209–32.

Zeitlyn, David. 2009. *Digital Anthropology Report.* Kent: University of Kent.

CHAPTER 6

Conclusion

Abstract This chapter provides an overall conclusion to the inquiry, and makes suggestions for further areas to research.

Keywords Digital communication · Face-to-face interactions · Technology · Language · Applied linguistics · Sociolinguistics

Although there is a very visible and valid argument about the way phones are negatively impacting face-to-face conversations, this book has tried to show that there is another side to this story. We do not always simply ignore or disconnect from others the moment we look at our phones, and in fact we may be using them to augment the conversation in ways that were not previously possible. Whilst there are negative aspects to this type of augmentation, there are also benefits. Furthermore, I have tried to show that augmenting our human abilities is a natural and normal part of our human ingenuity when it comes to creating tools and 'devolving responsibility' from our brains (Clark 2003, 25). Connectedness is part of augmented communication, as we can choose to use our phones to avoid engagement or get a short break. However, this is not necessarily exclusive and there is a gradient to how socially acceptable such types of discourse are. I have argued that context and personal relationships are vital for understanding augmented communication, just as they are for any other forms of linguistic analysis.

© The Author(s) 2019   123
R. S. Pinner, *Augmented Communication*,
https://doi.org/10.1007/978-3-030-02080-4_6

> Patterns of behaviour that traditionally existed in offline (physical) sociality are increasingly mixed with social and sociotechnical norms created in an online environment, taking on a new dimensionality. (van Dijck 2013, 19)

Connectedness can be attending to the talk and wanting to take it further by searching something ad hoc, but it is also possible to realise that the immediate conversation does not require a search in order to proceed. I would also like to make it clear that I am not attempting to undermine the work of scholars who have looked at the negative impact of digital technology on conversations, our society and mental health. I find much of this research very convincing, and I would like to make it clear that I do not propose that our current level of smartphone dependence is necessarily healthy or inherently either good or bad. I am, in fact, somewhat sceptical of the widespread use of phones, and I am particularly concerned about the existential consequences of being *always on* (Baron 2008). I find the work of people such as Sherry Turkle to be very rigorous, thought provoking and at the same time frightening. As a father myself, I feel I cannot ignore the potential danger that people would rather text than talk, where indicators of empathy are on the decline (Konrath et al. 2011), and where we are 'forever elsewhere' (Turkle 2015, 4). Therefore, although this book looks at the positive side of mobile networked digital devices on face-to-face communication, it does so within the wider context that there is a mounting debate about whether such devices are potentially having a negative influence on society. At the same time, there are arguments that take the opposite position, claiming that technology has the potential to enhance our capacity for empathy and expand it to a global scale. For example, Carolyn Calloway-Thomas (2010), whilst acknowledging that today's media can be a double-edged sword, claims that it also has the capacity to amplify empathy and extend our sense of unity to those who might otherwise be beyond our emotional and experiential landscape. Furthermore, several of the studies conducted by scholars such as dana boyd have shown that today's youths are not apathetic or disconnected, but that their efforts are simply underplayed by mainstream media (see for example boyd 2014, 206–11). Rather than disconnecting people, it has been argued that SNSs 'expand niche communities' (boyd and Ellison 2007, 218). Even some of the deplorable antics of online trolls can be viewed as offering an 'implicit critique' of mainstream media and capitalist business practices which profit from disasters and the grief of others (Phillips 2015, 6).

Although he acknowledges the arguments against technology and its potential impact on the millennial generation, Rifkin (2009) argues also that technology has the potential to spread empathic understanding across societies and ameliorate some of the impending environmental and economic crises that humanity faces. Furedi (2015) also argues against the claim that technology is decreasing our ability to focus, citing several historical arguments about the dangers of distraction. His argument is essentially that the fears that we are living in an age of distraction are not new, and thus the present argument is merely part of an ongoing discourse in which people voice concern about younger generations and modern technologies. Reminding us that 'new technology' is a relative term, Marvin (1988) has also shown in her study the general trepidation and mistrust that was voiced in popular media against such devices as the telephone. The warnings that this new technology could negatively impact society and the way people relate to each other is of course echoed in modern discourse now about smartphones and internet usage, just as it was for television and computer games more when they were relatively new (Greenfield 1984). Other common claims, such as how texting and online writing is impairing young people's linguistic ability, have also been rebutted by linguists (Crystal 2001; Tagg 2015). In an online interview, Professor of Logic and Metaphysics Andy Clark, points out that the argument that these technologies are changing us and making us less intelligent is somewhat reductive. He explains that the 'us' being referred to is only a small biological piece of a larger system, a more holistic understanding of ourselves as humans (Rheingold 2012). As Van Dijk (2012) has eloquently said, rather than creating change, technology merely amplifies ongoing changes. Making tools and creating new technologies is an essential aspect of our human nature, with language itself being a very ancient and exemplary case in point.

In pointing out the positive side of the use of phones in human interactions amid the rise of the network society, and in particular the intersection between face-to-face and networked communication, I do not intend to position myself as being aligned to any particular camp, but rather to simply describe observations that I have made as an applied linguist about how we use our phones in ways that could be seen to have an enhancing effect within the conversation.

6.1   Directions for Future Research

The book ends with a discussion of the way research could be undertaken into the phenomenon of augmented communication. Areas discussed include the neurological effect of augmented communication on working memory and cognitive load, the need for qualitative investigations relating to critical thinking and wider patterns of social patterns of interaction. Although a cautionary tone is used, research should also be carried out into how augmented communication also enhances face-to-face interaction.

One aspect that I have only briefly touched upon in this book is the digital divide, which is a further complex issue but very much implicated in the rise of augmented communication as a developing strategy of discourse in countries with high smartphone permeation. Clearly, smartphones are a sign of developed or developing technological societies, which in turn generally infers a degree of financial wealth, education and literacy, as well as social capital more generally. The digital divide exists not just between nations, but also within societies at various levels of the social hierarchy. It was slightly beyond the remit of this book to examine such inequalities in detail, although I did point out during the methodology section that my observations are based on people with whom I would ordinarily come into contact with. As a white, male, mid-30s associate professor at a Japanese university, this implies that I have attained a certain privileged position in society and likewise my friends and family will be in a similar position. Although this study presents a diverse range of people, most of them are educators or in education at the tertiary level, and as such I was unable to examine the digital divide or look at how augmented communication affects those at different tiers of society. Clearly, this is an area in need of further research, and it is most likely to an urgent area for inquiry.

Another area for deeper research would be into the effects of online discussions then blending into offline talk, and the way that these CMC and digital discourse lay down schematics for discourse which can be later picked up on within face-to-face conversation. I have also identified that further research into how augmented communication intersects with identity and its effect on social ties would be an area in which to explore further. It may also be that further categories of augmented communication may arise through further study, and thus other research designs which look at larger groups or target specific types of people may also provide insights into the way people use mobile networked devices during face-to-face interactions.

It seems that there are many avenues to further explore with regard to this recent and yet seemingly pervasive phenomenon. This book has presented an initial inquiry which identifies augmented communication as quite widespread in the contexts where I have observed it. It appears to be a naturally occurring novel utilisation of smartphones and other digital devices to enhance face-to-face interactions through various methods. I have shown how interlocutors augment conversations using multi-modal input, how we talk about digital technologies and digital culture whilst demonstrating in real time, how we use exomemory to expand conversations or make plans on the fly, and how we add other participants through various methods. This work's primary aim was to identify this issue and the ways augmented communication occurs in context, and to highlight further areas for study. With this done, I sincerely hope that more people will begin to reflect on how mobile networked technologies are influencing our face-to-face interactions, and the various consequences (both positive and negative) that occur as a result.

REFERENCES

Baron, Naomi S. 2008. *Always on: Language in an Online and Mobile World*. Oxford: Oxford University Press.
boyd, danah. 2014. *It's Complicated: The Social Lives of Networked Teens*. New Haven, CT: Yale University Press.
boyd, danah, and Nicole B. Ellison. 2007. "Social Network Sites: Definition, History, and Scholarship." *Journal of Computer-Mediated Communication* 13 (1): 210–30. https://doi.org/10.1111/j.1083-6101.2007.00393.x.
Calloway-Thomas, Carolyn. 2010. *Empathy in the Global World: An Intercultural Perspective*. London: Sage.
Clark, Andy. 2003. *Natural-Born Cyborgs: Minds, Technologies, and the Future of Human Intelligence*. New York: Oxford University Press.
Crystal, David. 2001. *Language and the Internet*. Cambridge: Cambridge University Press.
Furedi, Frank. 2015. "Age of Distraction: Why the Idea Digital Devices Are Destroying Our Concentration and Memory Is a Myth." *The Independent*, October 11. http://www.independent.co.uk/life-style/gadgets-and-tech/features/age-of-distraction-why-the-idea-digital-devices-are-destroying-our-concentration-and-memory-is-a-a6689776.html.

Greenfield, Patricia M. 1984. *Mind and Media: The Effects of Television, Video Games, and Computers, The Developing Child*. Cambridge, MA: Harvard University Press.

Konrath, Sara H., Edward H. O'Brien, and Courtney Hsing. 2011. "Changes in Dispositional Empathy in American College Students Over Time: A Meta-Analysis." *Personality and Social Psychology Review* 15 (2): 180–98.

Marvin, Carolyn. 1988. *When Old Technologies Were New: Thinking about Electric Communication in the Late Nineteenth Century*. Oxford: Oxford University Press.

Phillips, Whitney. 2015. *This Is Why We Can't Have Nice Things: Mapping the Relationship Between Online Trolling and Mainstream Culture*. Cambridge, MA: MIT Press.

Rheingold, Howard. 2012. Andy Clark on the Extended Mind. *YouTube*.

Rifkin, Jeremy. 2009. *The Empathic Civilization: The Race to Global Consciousness in a World in Crisis*. New York, NY: Jeremy P. Teacher/Penguin.

Tagg, Caroline. 2015. *Exploring Digital Communication: Language in Action*. London: Routledge.

Turkle, Sherry. 2015. *Reclaiming Conversation: The Power of Talk in a Digital Age*. New York: Penguin Press.

van Dijck, José. 2013. *The Culture of Connectivity: A Critical History of Social Media*. New York: Oxford University Press.

Van Dijk, Jan. 2012. *The Network Society*, 3rd ed. London: Sage.

INDEX

A

age, 10, 53–56, 71, 89, 92, 96, 105, 112, 125
Agger, Ben, 42
Apps, 37, 63
Argentina, 34, 36, 52, 77, 106, 108, 109
Audience, 30, 33, 39, 59, 76, 78
augmented cognition, 4, 7, 9, 15, 17, 18, 35, 38, 43, 49, 71–74, 93
augmented participation, 15, 35
authenticity, 41

B

boyd, danah, 9, 33, 35, 40, 41, 81, 124
brain, 22, 26, 32, 33, 73–75, 91, 93, 98, 99

C

Castells, Manuel, 30, 32
cognition. *See* augmented cognition
Confirmation bias, 102
connectedness, 104, 123, 124

connection, 14, 64, 75, 89, 96
consumer, 5, 32, 52, 88
context collapse, 9, 35, 56, 77, 81, 112
Convergence culture, 6, 10, 50
Critical thinking, 89, 100, 116, 126
culture, 5, 14, 30, 32, 33, 52, 70, 74, 107, 109
cyberbullying, 67
cyberstalking, 67

D

Digital culture, 42, 65, 69, 88, 127
Digital flâneurs, 81
digital literacy, 42, 89, 95, 116
Digital native, 80, 81. *See also* Millennial
Dumb, 96, 97, 103

E

Education, 31, 53, 90, 92, 102, 109, 126
Einstein, 92, 96, 98
Empathy, 2, 17, 25, 40, 62, 113, 124

© The Editor(s) (if applicable) and The Author(s) 2019
R. S. Pinner, *Augmented Communication*,
https://doi.org/10.1007/978-3-030-02080-4

Etiquette, 38, 51, 55, 60, 67, 103–105, 107–110
Exomemory, 3, 5, 7, 9, 14, 18, 39, 43, 49, 57, 60, 62, 63, 71, 72, 74–76, 92–94, 96, 127
Extrovert, 92

F
Facebook, 30, 33, 38, 39, 42, 52, 61, 62, 65–67, 70, 74, 77–79, 94, 113
friends, 66
like, 66
fake news, 100
false dichotomy, 1, 29, 39, 42
Friend, 8, 10, 12–15, 40, 42, 43, 51–54, 56, 61, 62, 64, 66, 67, 77–79, 81, 93–95, 109, 114, 126

G
generation, 33, 81, 96, 103, 104, 112–114, 125
Google, 1, 7, 14, 43, 57, 63, 71, 74, 75, 94
gossip, 67

H
Hawking, Stephen, 2, 22–24, 26, 27
Hong Kong, 66

I
Identity, 8–10, 23, 26, 35, 39, 41, 42, 55, 56, 64, 71, 74, 81, 88, 96, 110, 126
Images, 14, 34, 36, 50, 51, 53, 55–57, 59, 62, 64, 68, 71, 94, 101, 114

immediate authenticity, 43
Information, 3, 7, 8, 14, 16, 30, 31, 39, 43, 57, 60, 62, 63, 68, 73–76, 80, 89, 91–96, 98–100, 102, 115, 116
Intelligence, 32, 75, 97–100, 116
Italy, 105

J
Japan, 11, 39, 61, 70, 76, 79, 95, 97, 102, 107, 108

L
Language, 2, 3, 9, 10, 15–17, 22, 24, 26, 52, 67, 70, 88, 94, 96, 99, 101, 105, 107, 108, 125
Language (foreign language), 52, 90, 99
Like, 25, 30, 37, 39, 63
location, 7, 43, 77

M
McGurk, 90, 91
Media, 3, 5, 6, 8, 10, 16, 25, 30–32, 34, 36, 42, 49, 50, 52, 60, 61, 63, 65–70, 74, 77, 79, 81, 89, 91, 100–103, 107, 114, 116, 124, 125
Meme, 51, 68, 69, 92
Memory, 7, 16, 17, 36, 39, 52, 53, 61, 74, 90–94, 96, 98, 116
meta-augmenting, 15, 35
Meta-news, 68. *See also* news
Millennial, 125
mobile learning, 99
Multimodal, 8, 15, 17, 35, 49, 50, 52, 54, 55, 59, 60, 90, 91
Multitask, 5, 39

N
Natural born cyborgs, 7, 9, 75
Netiquette, 105, 109
networked society, 10, 30, 31, 56, 70, 78, 81
news, 68

O
Offline, 1, 5, 9, 12, 29, 30, 35, 39–42, 68, 77, 79, 101, 110, 112, 124, 126
Online, 1, 5, 7, 9, 11, 12, 14, 29, 30, 32, 35, 36, 39–43, 50, 56, 59, 62, 64–66, 69–71, 75, 77, 79, 81, 88, 89, 94, 95, 101, 105, 106, 110–112, 124, 125
Online vs offline. *See* false dichotomy

P
Photograph, 14, 34, 37, 42, 53, 79, 90, 110
Politeness, 105. *See also* Etiquette power, 105
Politics, 101
Polymedia, 6, 7, 9, 10
Polyreality, 112
Produser, 32

S
schema, 66
schemata, 79, 90
Seargeant, Philip, 8, 41, 42, 56, 96, 100
Share, 32, 57, 59, 63, 69, 71, 81, 101, 112, 114
Singapore, 66, 76
Skype, 3, 39, 78
Snippet literacy, 30
social anxiety, 66
social class, 89

Social Networking Services (SNS), 32, 34, 37, 41–43, 56, 59, 61, 64–66, 68, 70, 79, 80, 94, 102, 106, 124
Solidarity (female speech), 53
synchronous/asynchronous, 35, 39, 41, 43, 50, 66, 71, 77, 79

T
Tagg, Caroline, 1, 8, 32, 39, 41, 42, 56, 96, 100, 105, 125
Teaching, 108, 109
technological determinism, 97
Technology, 1, 2, 5–9, 14–18, 21–26, 30, 32, 33, 36, 37, 43, 49, 60, 62, 66, 72–74, 77, 78, 80, 88, 90–93, 97, 99, 109–111, 114–116, 124, 125, 127
Text, 6, 23, 24, 30, 32, 50, 52, 64, 68, 69, 74, 77, 79, 80, 88, 90, 108, 110, 115, 124
Thought contagion, 102
Transmedia, 10, 50
Transportable identity, 8, 9, 55, 56, 71
Turkle, Sherry, 2, 30, 32, 40, 41, 62, 64, 68, 71, 74–76, 80, 81, 103–105, 111, 112, 124
TV, 11, 12, 17, 36, 43, 59, 61, 63, 65, 102, 107, 125
Twitter, 30, 33, 38, 62, 65, 68, 70, 94, 114

U
UK, 24, 60, 70, 92, 96, 99–101, 109

V
Verbal, 3, 26, 52, 91, 110
Video, 3, 8, 23, 24, 26, 27, 35, 39, 50, 54–60, 63, 68, 77–79, 89, 91, 108, 111, 114

Viral, 3, 34, 35, 59, 63, 76, 111
Virtual, 111
Virtuality, 30
Voice, 2, 16, 17, 21–27, 31, 41, 77,
    88, 125
VOIP, 78

W
WhatsApp, 61, 64, 68, 104, 108
Wikipedia, 38, 39, 74
Workgroup, 38, 54, 55, 61, 62, 70,
    75, 76, 79, 103, 106, 110
Working memory, 75, 92–94, 96, 98,
    99, 116, 126

Writing, 5, 12, 16, 24, 26, 31, 36, 52,
    75, 80, 101, 111, 125

Y
Youth, 40, 70, 96, 114, 124
YouTube, 23, 57–59, 63, 111

Z
Zombie, 37, 114
Zombify, 36, 37